Flying Over
GAUDÍ

Text
Guida Alzina

Illustrations
Consol Escarrà

ediciones experiencia

All rights reserved. No part of this publication may be reproduced, stored in a retrieval system, or transmitted, in any form or by any means, electronic, mechanical, photocopying, recording, scanning or otherwise, without the permission in writing of the publisher.

First edition: April 2002

© Text, Guida Alzina
© Il.lustrations, Consol Escarrà

© EDICIONES EXPERIENCIA
   c/ Sant Eusebi 53, 1.º 2.ª
   08006 BARCELONA
   Tel.: 932 002 309   Fax: 932 413 129

I.S.B.N. 84-932264-4-0
Depósito Legal: B- 22.829-2002

Traduced by Julie Flanagan

Printed in Spain

Gràfiques 92, S.A.
Avda. Can Sucarrats 91; 08191 Rubí (Barcelona)

Prologue

Joan Bassegoda i Nonell
Director of the Gaudí Chair

There are many ways of contemplating Gaudí, from the mute admiration of little children who are enchanted and enthralled by the expressive power of stones that speak, cry or laugh. Then there is the erudite scrutiny of critics who normally do not understand anything and spend their time letting fly a few dialectical and intellectual pigeons.

What has been made to fly in this book is quite another kind of bird. A delightful sensitivity, a profound sense of poetry, exquisite pencil lines and watercolour brushwork have come together here in an ensemble that enraptures the reader and even the person who tends merely to flip through books.

Without pretensions to writing any kind of criticism or history, or even architectural history, the drawings, paintings and, in general, the felicitous combination of text and illustration, provide the most solid of foundations for the flight of this dove that sees Gaudí in a space somewhere between heaven and earth, far from the quarrels of men and close to the light of the sun that was the source of inspiration for Gaudí's architectural work.

This book makes Gaudí's architecture more comprehensible because its approach is discrete, humble and free of prejudice and a priori ideas.

The true sense of Gaudí's work is optimally present when it is experienced, inhaled and captured through feeling rather than by the intelligence.

This book takes the same approach, offering an exciting and sensitive vision of these piles of stones and bricks that have come together in one of the most fascinating poems in the history of art.

Introduction   Guida Alzina-Consol Escarrà

Flying over Gaudí is a book which has appeared neither by chance nor in response to any artistic fashion. It was born out of a desire to present, simply and naturally, the work of this universal architect. Perhaps we have wanted to offer the reader our admittedly very personal view of each of the Master's works because we love art and feel it in the depths of our beings.

From the very start, we have believed that, to reflect a work such as Gaudí's, we had to achieve a total approximation to its reality. Step by step, we have looked at every stone, every piece of ironwork, stained glass, mosaics . . . And we have tried, as much as we could, to enter into the complex personality of the artist.

It has not been easy to capture and comprehend a spirit so rebellious and contradictory as that of Antoni Gaudí. Yet it has been a beautiful, moving and enriching task.

By no means have we attempted to write a treatise on architecture but rather we have tried, in few words and sensitively and artistically, to approach the surprising and fantastic world that the architect-genius created.

Poetry and drawing have come together to undertake this pilgrimage. And we have expressed it through the flight of a dove, both inquisitive and artist, that has glimpsed this treasure from his bird's-eye view. A dove that has been able to discover in nature the spirit of Gaudí.

Index

Prologue   III
Introduction   V
Itinerary   IX
Some brief concepts of poetry   XIX
Formal structure of the poems or poetic compositions   XXI
Güell Park   2
Bellesguard   24
Teresian College   30
The houses   37
Casa Vicens   39
Casa Milà "La Pedrera"   42
Casa Batlló   47
Casa Calvet   51
Güell Palace   55
The lamp-posts   60
The Aribau balustrade   65
Cathedral. Palma de Mallorca   67
Can Artigues   69
Sagrada Familia, expiatory church   73
Pavilions at the Finca Güell   87
Entrance to the Finca Miralles   93
Colònia Güell Crypt   95
First Mystery of the Glory (Montserrat)   99
Güell Cellars (Garraf)   101
Casa de los Botines (León)   105
Episcopal Palace (Astorga)   115
El Capricho (Comillas – Santander)   123
Bibliography   137
Acknowledgements   139

Itinerary

GÜELL PARK   1900 – 1914

Polychrome mosaic work contrasts with the areas of viaducts, massive stone balconies and sinuous pathways. Gaudí succeeded here in a totally free fusion of art and nature, respecting the native plants of the area and creating a perfect and magical symbiosis. Notable is the tank that collects rainwater from the square, running it off through a system of Doric columns to a large collection area beneath the temple. It is said that the overflow outlet of the tank was the dragon's mouth. In 1984 Güell Park was included in the UNESCO World Heritage List.

Avda. del Carmel, no number. Parking space available
C/ d'Olot, no number. Barcelona. Telephone for information: 93 413 24 00
Hours: Winter — from 10 a.m. to 6 p.m. Summer – from 10 a.m. to 8 p.m.
GAUDÍ MUSEUM-HOUSE (the same hours). Telephone for information: 93 488 01 39
Buses: 24, 25 and Tourist Bus

BELLESGUARD   1900 – 1909

A free-standing house, of Gothic inspiration, this building is constructed in the slate-coloured stone of the surroundings over the ruins of the palace of King Martin the Humane. The stained-glass work in the centre of the building is interesting for its colours and its three-dimensional effects. At the top of the tower is the royal crown, the flag and the four-armed Greek cross. In the extraordinary attic, the arches and vaults with triangular fretwork are of exposed brick and majestic in their effect even though this space was conceived as servants' quarters.

C/ de Bellesguard, 16-20. Barcelona. Telephone for information: 93 211 56 90
Private property. To visit the gardens in summer, telephone 93 488 01 30
Bus 60 / FFCC (Railways of Catalonia): Bonanova station

TERESIAN COLLEGE   1887 – 1888

This building is like a castle of Gothic inspiration, with a great number of symbols of Saint Theresa and Carmel. The locks are designed in the form of a T and can only be opened from the inside. The parabolic arches of the first-floor passageway are one of the most brilliant features of this original construction.

C/ Ganduxer, 85. Barcelona. Telephone for information: 93 212 33 54
Private property of the Teresian Order

CASA VICENS   1883 – 1888

Gaudí was inspired by the yellow flowers and palmettos that were growing on the block before the construction of this oriental-style house began and he conceived for it a natural decorative style both inside and out.

c/ de les Carolines, 18-24. Barcelona. Private property
The garden is open to the public on Saint Rita's day, 22 May
Buses: 22, 24, 25, 27, 28, 31 and 32 and Tourist Bus. Metro: Line 3 Fontana station.

CASA MILÀ   1906   1912

This house is constructed on a block of more than a thousand square metres. The façades are constructed of Garraf stone on the ground floor while the upper floors are of Vilafranca stone with a rustic finish that gives rise to the name *La Pedrera* (The Quarry). Notable are the cast-iron work of the balconies, the roof terraces with their spectacular sculpted chimneys in stone and broken ceramic mosaic work. The attic area is now occupied by the *Espai Gaudí* (Gaudí Space) with models, videos and graphic documentation. UNESCO listed this building as World Heritage in 1984.

Passeig de Gràcia 92 – Provença 261. Barcelona
Telephone for information: 93 484 59 00
Hours: From 10 a.m. to 10 p.m. all year round. Closed 25 and 26 December and 6 January.
Buses: 22, 24, 28 and Tourist Bus. Metro: Lines 3 and 5, Diagonal station.

CASA BATLLÓ   1904 – 1906

The ground floor and first floor are constructed in Montjuïc stone sculpted in organic forms. The upper floors are decorated with coloured glass mosaic work. The mask-like balconies are of cast iron while the roof of the attic area resembles a dragon's flank. At the top of the tower is a four-armed Greek cross. Some of the first-floor windows are of stained and leaded glass.

c/ Passeig de Gràcia, 43. Barcelona. Telephone for information: 93 488 06 66
Hours: from 9 a.m. to 1.30 p.m.
Buses: 7, 10, 17, 22, 24, 28 and Tourist Bus. Metro: Lines 2, 3 and 4, Passeig de Gràcia station

CASA CALVET   1898

This house with its baroque air was awarded the prize for the best building constructed in 1900. The façade is of Montjuïc stone and the balconies have lobulated railings. The entrance hall with its Solomonic columns is outstanding, as are the lift of iron, wood and glass and the large knocker on the entrance door in the form of a cross which repeatedly crushes an evil insect in a symbolic representation of the struggle between good and evil.

c/ Casp, 48. Barcelona. Telephone for information: 93 488 01 39
Buses, 16, 17, 22, 28, 39, 42, 45, 47 and 55. Metro: Lines 3 and 4. Plaça Urquinaona station
Nowadays there is a restaurant on the ground floor

GÜELL PALACE   1886 – 1888

The marble that was used for constructing the palace was brought from the Garraf massif. The entrance, with its double doorway of parabolic arches, is of cast-iron filigree work, as is the central window that bears the shield of Catalonia that doubled as the grille of the concierge's office. In the basement area, originally stables, the three-layered Catalan vaults are notable. The cylindrical columns, some with inverted conical capitals, the pillars and the ceiling are of exposed brickwork. The hall is at the very the centre of the building, its ceiling a parabolic cupola, where the light enters through small orifices creating a starred effect. Luxury is evident in all the materials used, from the exotic woods, beaten copper, ivory, inlay work and cast-iron work. The roof terrace is of two levels with twenty chimneys of different forms and a conical central tower surrounded by four skylights. UNESCO listed this building as World Heritage in 1984.

c/ Nou de la Rambla, 3-5. Barcelona. Telephone for information: 93 317 39 74
Hours: Monday to Saturday from 10 a.m. to 2 p.m. and 4 p.m. to 8 p.m..
Closed Sundays and public holidays
Buses: 14, 18, 38, 48 and 59. Metro: Line 3, Liceu station

LAMP-POSTS, PLAÇA REIAL
LAMP-POSTS, PLA DE PALAU   1879 – 1890

The lamp-posts in the Plaça Reial have six branches while, in the Pla de Palau, they have three, with stone bases and lamps of bronze, iron and glass.

Plaça Reial. Barcelona. Metro: Line 3, Liceu station
Plaça Palau. Opposite the Civil Governor's building. Bus: 39. Metro: Line 4, Barceloneta station.

CIUTADELLA PARK
IRON FENCE, ARIBAU BALUSTRADE, AQUARIUM   1876 – 1882

Notable are the iron fence surrounding the park and the ornamental lamp-posts at the three entrance gates, along with the stone balustrade surrounding the bust of Aribau to enclose a small square.
The aquarium, now no longer in use, has two notable medallions, in stone relief work with vegetable and animal symbolism, on the wall at each side of the entrance.

Passeig de Pujades. Barcelona
Bus: 39. Metro: Line 4, Barceloneta station

MALLORCA CATHEDRAL   1903 – 1914

The interior of the Cathedral, with Gaudí's liturgical restoration, houses a major collection of works in ceramic, wood, iron and glass. In the sacristy is a curious small bell with a sun at the top and, while its design is simple, it has surprising sonority.

Plaça Almoina, no number. Palma de Mallorca
Telephone for information: 97 172 31 30. Tourist Office of Palma: 97 172 40 90

CAN ARTIGUES
Magnesium Fountain   1904

Near the Artigues factory and in a narrow valley of the Llobregat River, Gaudí designed a natural garden with stones, water and vegetation. Noteworthy are the grotto made with large uncut stones and, next to it, the Magnesium Fountain which gives the gardens its more popular name. The river passes between large pots, arches made of crudely hewn stone and under a bridge with railings formed in local cement to resemble tree trunks. Further along the path is an arched bridge with steps leading up to a cylindrical summerhouse with a roof made of scree. The Gaudí Chair supervised the recent restoration of these gardens at la Pobla de Lillet.

La Pobla de Lillet (Berguedà region). Telephone for information: 93 823 61 46
Visiting hours: Saturdays, 11 a.m. to 6 p.m.. Sundays and holidays, 11 a.m. to 2 p.m.
Between July and September, visiting hours are from 11 a.m. to 8 p.m. every day.

BOCABELLA ORATORY   1885
This private chapel has an altar made of wood and woven materials.

c/ Ausias Marc, 31. Barcelona
Private property. May not be visited

SANT PACIÀ CHURCH   1879

Gaudí's design of a magnificent floor in Roman mosaic style with geometric borders.

Sant Pacià Parish
C/ del Vallès, 40. Sant Andreu de Palomar district
May be visited from 5 p.m. to 8 p.m., with due respect for religious services.
Buses: 3, 35 and 40. Metro: Line 1, Fabra i Puig station

SAGRADA FAMILIA   1883 – 1926

Gaudí's greatest work, where construction began with the crypt, the apse and the Nativity façade. Gaudí worked 43 years on this project, leaving a complete drawing for the Passion façade and a preliminary version of the Glory façade. A plaster model of the whole construction, to a scale of 1 to 25, is conserved. In his work on the expiatory church of the Sagrada Família, Gaudí developed his theory of architecture along with a meticulous study of liturgy and religious expression. In the final years of his life he lived in the workshop.

Plaça Sagrada Família, c/ Mallorca, 403 – c/ Provença, 450 – c/ Marina, 253. Barcelona
Telephone for information: 93 207 30 31
Metro: Lines 2 and 3, Sagrada Família station.

PROVISIONAL CLASSROOMS   1909

While this is a lesser work, a simple and economical construction, in Gaudí's hands it is a masterly lesson in architecture where, as in nature, each element, in terms of its material, form and construction, is the most appropriate for its function. The building consists of three classrooms in a row with windows from one side to the other. Three pillars sustain the conoid surface of the roof, giving it the characteristic undulation that distinguishes this singular building.

Inside the Sagrada Família precincts – Passion façade. c/ Mallorca, 403. Barcelona
The possibility of moving it 30 metres and subsequently restoring it is presently being studied.

GÜELL PAVILIONS
(FINCA GÜELL)   1884 – 1887

Oriental in style and constructed in exposed brickwork with a finish of enamelled tiles and broken ceramic mosaic-work, one pavilion was designed as the entrance building while the other was to be used for the stable hands. The building is now the premises of the Gaudí Chair. Particularly notable is the carriage entrance, an exceptional gate worked in cast iron to represent a dragon.

Headquarters of the Gaudí Chair, archives and library
Avda. Pedralbes, 7. Barcelona. Telephone for information: 93 204 52 50
Visiting hours: every morning after consultation with Professor Joan Bassegoda i Nonell's office.
Buses: 6, 7, 16, 63, 67, 68, 74, 75, 78 and the Tourist Bus.
Metro: Line 3, Palau Reial or Maria Cristina stations

HERCULES FOUNTAIN
(FINCA GÜELL)   1884 – 1887

Located in the Pedralbes gardens, this fountain, topped with a bust of Hercules, originally Greek but presently Roman, has another cast-iron dragon as its spout, while the water falls into the bowl of the fountain to run across the shield of Catalonia, the four bars of which run off the overflow.

Gardens of the Pedralbes Palace. Barcelona
Hours: 10 a.m. to 7 p.m. Metro: Line 3, Palau Reial station

SECONDARY ENTRANCE
(FINCA GÜELL)   1884 – 1887

Once one of the entrances to the Finca Güell, it now gives access to the Faculty of Pharmacy. It is constructed in exposed bricks and tiles glazed in deep red and white.

Avda. Joan XXIII. Barcelona
Metro: Line 3, Maria Cristina or Palau Reial stations

ENTRANCE TO THE FINCA MIRALLES   1900 - 1902

This dry-stone wall with bulging forms is crowned by an undulating top that is protected by an ornamental metal layer. An iron shelter covers the main entrance.

c/ Manuel Girona, 55. Barcelona

CRYPT AT THE COLÒNIA GÜELL   1908

Magnificent crypt with slanted columns, flat-laid brickwork vaults in irregular forms. Stained glass windows in the form of flowers, with an ingenious mechanism whereby pulling on a fine chain from one of the windows makes the glass seem to flutter like a butterfly's wing.
This work of Gaudí's is magical, both inside and out. It is worth making the trip to see it.

c/ Reixach, no number. Santa Coloma de Cervelló. Baix Llobregat region (15 Km from Barcelona)
Telephone for information: 93 685 24 00
Hours: Sundays from 8 a.m. to 1 p.m.

MONTSERRAT
FIRST MYSTERY OF THE GLORY   1903

Excavation of an eastwards-looking grotto with an ornamental mosaic shield of Catalonia.

Camí de la Cova (Path to the Cave). Montserrat
Barcelona – Igualada road
Bus: Julià company leaving from Plaça Països Catalans (Sants Station)
Telephone for information Monastery of Montserrat: 93 835 02 01

GÜELL CELLARS   1895 – 1897

This is a triangular-shaped building with two large basement areas and a chapel in its uppermost part. Garraf stone is used in its construction. Notable is an iron chain-mesh door.

At the 25 Km turnoff on the Barcelona-Sitges road appearing on the sign as Restaurant Gaudí-Garraf.
Spanish Railways: Line C2 (Granollers – Vilanova), Garraf station
Bus line MON-BUS: Leaving from the Ronda de la Universitat stop, Barcelona
By car: Road 246, Costes del Garraf

CASA DE LOS BOTINES   1892 – 1894

This house has a stone façade and four corner towers with Gothic and medieval influences and a slate-tiled attic roof. The Catalan vault was introduced into the León region with this building. There is a remarkable piece of ironwork fencing surrounding the lower ground floor.

Plaza de San Marcelo, 5. León
Only the ground floor may be visited. Telephone for information: 98 789 55 03
Bank property

EPISCOPAL PALACE OF ASTORGA   1889 – 1893

Constructed of Bierzo granite, its lower ground floor (like that of the Casa de los Botines) is illuminated by light entering from the moat surrounding the building, which gives the appearance of a medieval fortress-castle. Notable in its interior are the vaults in flat-laid brickwork, with veins in the deep-red glazed ceramic that is typical of the town of Jiménez de Jamuz.

c/ Glorieta Eduardo de Castro, no number. Astorga (León), next to the Cathedral
The Palace houses the "Caminos" (Santiago pilgrims' route) Museum
Telephone for information: 98 761 53 50

EL CAPRICHO   1883 – 1885

Building in worked stone at the lower level with brickwork and ceramic tiles at the upper levels. A high cylindrical tower accentuates its oriental air. The exterior sash windows are musical, thanks to a number of gadgets such as chimes, metal sheets, tubular pipes and lead counterweights. A folly. The most important decorative element is the sunflower tiles with embossed green leaves

Barrio de Sobrellano, no number. Comillas (Santander).
Telephone for information: 94 272 07 68
The building is presently the property of the Restaurant El Capricho de Gaudí
Hours: the gardens are open to visitors. Restaurant telephone: 94 272 03 65

THE MATARÓ WORKERS' COOPERATIVE   1974 – 1885

Whitewashed hall with wooden catenary-profiled arches. Presently being restored.

c/ Cooperativa, near the RENFE (Railway) station
To arrange a visit telephone the Mataró Town Council on: 93 758 21 00

ALTAR AND MONSTRANCE   1879

Alabaster altar and wooden monstrance with metal hinges. The chapel presently belongs to the Archdiocese of Tarragona.

Capella de la Mare de Déu del Sagrat Cor
c/ Méndez Núñez, 23. Tarragona. Telephone for information: 97 723 34 12

SANTÍSSIM (HOLY SACRAMENT) CHAPEL, ALELLA
Project of 1883

Project on cloth paper, with neo-Gothic influences. It is conserved in the parish archive of Alella.

Saint Felix Parish Church of Alella
Plaça de l'Ajuntament, no number. Alella (El Maresme)
Telephone for information: 93 555 23 91

Some brief concepts of poetry

Starting from the idea that ART is the same as FREEDOM, I understand that not everyone has the same idea of freedom.

The meanings of this word over history have been, and still may be, classified according to a range of tendencies, generations, evolutions and periods.

I therefore take the liberty of offering a highly schematic and personal view of what I think is essential to a poetic work.

I don't mean to say that others who might think differently are wrong.

> *Any written work, be it verse or prose, must bear a message in order to awaken interest. In poetry, which is what concerns us now, we call this the poetic message.*

What is a poetic message?

A poem is like an open letter that describes facts or events through feeling.

The aim of a poem is to awaken, through the word, different feelings by means of an emotional stimulus that will move those who receive it.

Poetry-art only exists when there exists this possibility for such a transmission.

Any poem, be it short or long, must contain a complete synthesis of the idea it presents. Thus, I think the beginning and the end of a poem are the two most important parts.

The beginning is to awaken interest. The end pulls it all together so as not to disappoint.

POETRY IN GENERAL	The harmonic perception of beauty
A POEM	The written expression of a feeling that might awaken other related feelings, using as its vehicles words and (whatever) verse form.
VERSE	There are three main meanings: (1) a line of metrical writing; (2) a stanza; and (3) poetry in general.
STROPHE	Groups of a particular number of lines into which a poem is divided.
STRUCTURE	The formal or plastic appearance of a poem.
RHYME	Equal or similar sounds ending a verse (in the first sense).
METER	The number and pattern of stressed and unstressed syllables in each verse (first sense).
RHYTHM	The harmonic movement or sense of movement conveyed by the arrangement of stressed and unstressed syllables, or metrical pattern.

Outline

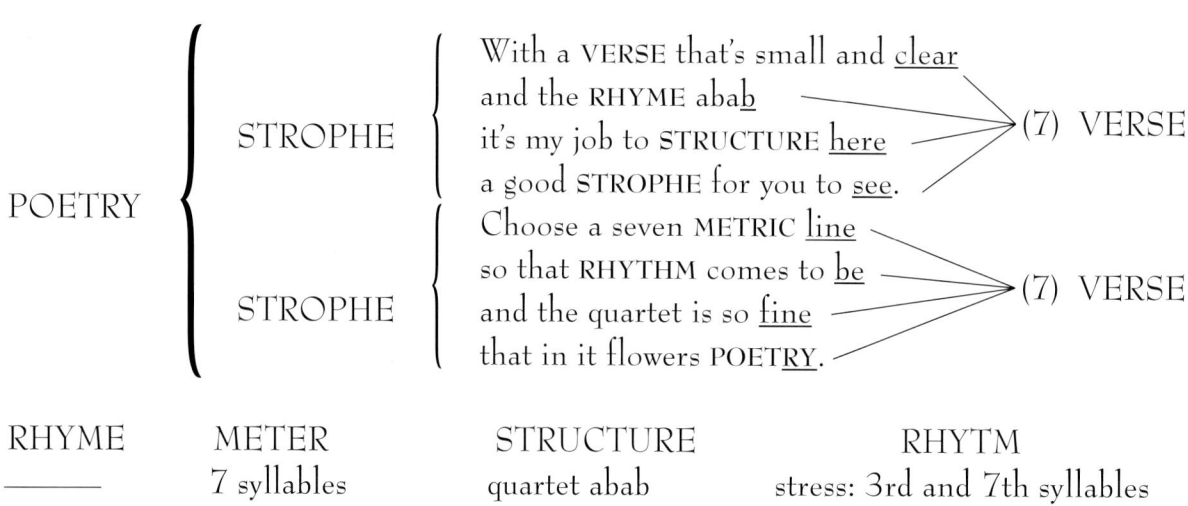

RHYME	METER	STRUCTURE	RHYTM
———	7 syllables	quartet abab	stress: 3rd and 7th syllables

Formal structure of poems or poetic compositions

ACROSTIC — A composition used by the troubadours (11th century). The first letter of each line, read from top to bottom, forms a phrase. The strophes adapt to the word, name or phrase chosen (page 109).

ALTAR POEM — A stanza formed by a series of lines free in metrics and disposition. Believed to have been created by Persian poets, it was much used in Italy especially during the Renaissance. If the composition has more than one stanza, the first serves as the model for the rest. The stanza here is of opposing and symmetrical rhyme. (page 96).

BALLAD ("arte menor") — Composition of *arte menor* verses where all the even-numbered (*"minor art"*) lines rhyme (assonant or consonant) and the rest are free or unrhymed (page 104).

BLANK VERSE — This verse form has meter but is unrhymed. Blank or free verse can be grouped in poetic compositions forming continuous series or a single strophe. Depending on the poet, it may be divided into stanzas (page 31).

CLASSICAL OCTAVE — An eight-line stanza with two or three rhymes. Also known in Old Provençal as a "Cobla" (page 78).

CLASSICAL TERZINA — This is a combination of three lines, all three, or two of them, united by a single rhyme. The free-standing verse in the middle rhymes with the first and third lines of the following terzina to form a composition of indeterminate length with a cauda at the end that is the determinant of all the rhymes. It became popular with Dante's <u>La Divina Commedia</u> (page 116).

COBLA ("arte mayor") — Attributed to the Cordoba poet Juan de Mena, though it seems the its real creator was the Galician poet Xulian Bolseiro, this is an 8-line strophe with a decasyllable (10 syllables) meter and central caesura (5 + 5). *Arte mayor* ("major art"), is a Spanish form dating from the 13th century, bringing a new seriousness to Spanish poetry (page 71).

CODOLADA — A Catalan form (13th and 14th centuries) of couplets with a different number of syllables. It can begin with an 8-syllable couplet and then move on to an alternating tetrasyllabic (4-syllable) form and an octosyllabic (8 syllable) form (page 13).

"CODOLINA" — A form derived from the codolada and created at the "Living Poetry Research Seminar" in Catalonia. It follows the codolada scheme with a meter of 4 to 8 syllables, though differs in that the distichs do not form couplets. The "ina" suffix refers to the rhyming between strophes (page 39).

COUPLET — A two-line rhyming verse (page 6).

"DECÀMERA" (neologism) — A ten-line strophe. This dècamara is couplets in *arte menor* ("minor

XXI

	art"), a Spanish form used for popular verse (page 114).
DÉCIMA OR ESPINELLA	A Spanish composition of heptasyllabic (7 syllables) lines attributed to Vicente Espinel and highly favoured by fabulists. It has 10 lines and four rhymes, usually abba:accddc (page 64).
"DISTINE"	This neologism refers to a form derived from the distich form (two-line strophe from classical poetry) and created at the "Living Poetry Research Seminar" in Catalonia. The distine is a composition of rhymed distichs, usually ending in a cauda (from the Latin: tail) (page 18).
ENGLISH MORPHOSONNET (ballad)	Derived from the Greek "*morfo*" this poem has the form of the sonnet, as the name suggests. It can be any poem of different structures that respects the basic sonnet form. The adjective "English" reflects the structural variant used by Shakespeare for his sonnets (page 41).
EPIGRAM	A brief composition to express a specific thought usually witty, surprising and condensed. Its origins are in Greek and Latin lyric poetry (300 BC) (page 21).
ESPLUGUESIAN STANZA (neologism)	Or sometimes, Esplugasian strophe – this is based on a quintet in which the first and second lines are octosyllabic (eight syllables) and always with a central stress. The third and fourth lines are tetrasyllabic (4 syllables) and the fifth octosyllabic. There is no caesura. The endings of the first line are always feminine (in Spanish) and unrhymed. The second line is masculine and rhymed with the fifth, the third and fourth form a couplet of feminine ending. The creator of this form is Josep Esplugues i Bator, whence its name (page 93).
FRENCH PANTUN (neologism)	This composition consists of three or four connected rhymed quartets. The second and fourth lines of each form the first and third lines of the next quartet. The final verse is independent but the last line repeats the first line of the initial verse. The form was created by a number of 11th-century French poets on the basis of a very free interpretation of the Malay pantun (page 74).
GREEK FEET (amphibrach)	Units formed by a set of syllables (page 43). (Amphibrach: one unstressed syllable, one stressed and one unstressed [∪ / ∪]).
GREEK FEET (anapaests)	Units formed by a set of syllables (page 11). (Anapaest: two unstressed and one stressed syllables [∪ ∪ /]).
GREEK FEET (iambic)	Units formed by a set of syllables (page 59). (Iambic: one unstressed syllable and one stressed [∪ /]).
HAIKU	A brief, subtle and concise Japanese composition in which 17 syllables are distributed as follows: five in the first line, seven in the second line and five in the third line. This is blank (unrhymed) verse with unstressed word endings (page 24).
"HEPTAMERA" (neologism)	Seven-line strophes (page 89).
ITALIAN OCTAVE	This is an eight-line strophe with its origins in Occitaine or Provençal metrics. In the Middle Ages it was known as a *cobla*. After the 14th century new schemes from Italy were introduced, for example the

	Italian octave with three sets of rhymed lines and two blank (unrhymed) (page 60).
LYRICAL OCTAVE	This is similar to the Italian octave and it is presumed to be Italian by origin although it is not mentioned as such in texts on poetry. Like other octaves, it is formed by a rhyming scheme of ababcccb (page 69).
MADRIGAL	Brief poem often formed by two or three tercets and ending with a refrain. Preferably decasyllable (10-syllable line) and hexasyllable (6-syllable line), its content was usually amorous. Italian Renaissance in origin (page 27).
MALAYSIAN PANTUN	A traditional Malaysian form. The meter is not specified and the rhyming scheme is abab with the distinguishing feature that *the first two lines have no relation with the last two. The first two are only there for rhyming purposes while the last two lines are those that pertain to the theme of the pantun* (page 53).
MONO-RHYMED QUATRAIN OR *CUADERNA VIA*	Medieval quartet, used by Ramon Llull amongst others. It is also known as *cuaderna vía* (in Spanish: quaternary manner) or Alexandrine monorhymed tretrastrophe (13th-century *mestre de clerecía* (art of the clerics) with Alexandrine verses) This is a four-line strophe with a single rhyme (page 118).
NINE-LINE STANZA	A strophe with nine lines (page 123).
OMAR KHAYYÁM OR PERSIAN QUARTET	A four-line composition where three lines (1,2 and 4) rhyme and the third is blank. The meter is decasyllabic (10 syllables). Its origin, as the name suggests, is Persian and it was specifically used by the

	poet Omar Khayýam (pages 56 and 101).
QUATRAIN ("envelope stanza")	A four-line strophe or quartet with rhyming between the first and fourth lines and the second and third, or an abba scheme (page 9).
QUATRAIN (abab scheme)	A four-line strophe or quartet where the first and third and second and fourth lines rhyme (page 48).
QUATRAIN WITH CAUDATE RHYME	A four-line strophe or quartet with rhymed first and second lines and then third and fourth, or an aabb rhyming scheme (page 47).
"QUARTINE" (neologism)	A composition of quatrains totally joined by rhyme with a characteristic cauda that determines the whole composition in bringing it all together. This form was created in Catalonia at the "Living Poetry Research Seminar" (page 98).
QUINTAIN	A five-line strophe otherwise known as a quintet (page 76).
QUINTET	A five-line strophe otherwise known as a quintain (page 5).
"QUINTINE" (neologism)	A composition of five-line strophes joined by rhyme with a cauda or closing verse. This form was created in Catalonia at the "Living Poetry Research Seminar" (page 87).
ROYAL OCTAVE	This, like the Italian octave, is of Italian origin, and formed by six lines with an alternating rhyming scheme (abab) and a final couplet (page 62).
SAPPHIC ODE	This is a very beautiful and sonorous strophe based on a quartet with three Sapphic verses (stress on first, fourth and eighth syllables), always ending with an unstressed syllable. In decasyllables (10 sylla-

	bles), it consists of an adonic line (a dactyl followed by a spondee, ending with an unstressed syllable). There is no rhyme in classical Sapphic odes. This composition was created by the famous poetess Sappho (6th to 7th century BC) of the island of Lesbos. The ode was modified by the poet Horace (1st century BC) and adapted to a later meter (page 45).
SEXAIN	A six-line strophe with great diversity in its rhyming scheme (page 51).
SHAKESPEARIAN SONNET	Sonnet created by Shakespeare based on three quatrains of independent rhyme and a final couplet (page 72).
SILVA	A Spanish form of alternating hexasyllabic or decasyllabic (or heptasyllabic and hendasyllabic) alternating lines with a variable rhyming scheme (page 107).
SONG WITH PARALLELISM	Provençal in origin, this composition is very similar to the Zéjel. Its name derives from the fact that different words are used to repeat the same idea (page 34).
"SONINA" (neologism)	A sonnet totally linked by its rhyme where the terzina technique is applied. It has fifteen lines because a determining cauda is added, bringing together all the previous lines. This form was created in Catalonia at the "Living Poetry Research Seminar"(page 94).
SONNET	Composition of 14 lines distributed as two quartets and two tercets. The sonnet is regarded as the perfect poem for its technical precision (page 23).
SONNET (*arte menor*)	This is a sonnet in *arte menor* form (page 85).
SONNET WITH ESTRAMBOTE	The structure is essentially that of a sonnet. The estrambote is a Spanish form involving the addition of a few lines at the end of a poem. It is most commonly a tercet linked by rhyme with the last line of a sonnet and it often begins with a hexasyllabic line (page 82).
STORNELLO	An Italian (from Tuscany) folk verse form of three lines beginning with an invocation of a flower or plant (page 14).
TANKA	A brief composition, Japanese in origin, consisting of a five-line strophe divided into 31 syllables according to the following scheme; 5-7-5-7-7. Each line must end with an unstressed syllable. It may be seen as an extension of the Haiku form (pages 90-91).
TERZINA (with fourth paeons)	A three-line strophe with fourth paeons (a Greek foot consisting of three unstressed syllables and one stressed ($\cup \cup \cup /$) (page 67).
TRI-SONNET OR TRINITARY SONNET (neologism)	These are sonnets with broken lines. The first set forms a sonnet with the same rhyming scheme as the second, but they are independent of each other. The union of these two sonnets come together to create a third of unforced and coherent text. The three different readings of a single sonnet justify the name of tri-sonnet (page 125).
TRISTICH WITH CAUDA (OR DANCE)	Composition formed by a refrain (normally a couplet) leading in and followed by three tercets with a single rhyme, each completed by a fourth verse that rhymes with the refrain. This is called the cauda. This form is Provençal in origin (page 33).

VILLANELLE   Pastoral composition usually set to music, a folk form in opposition to the more literary madrigal. According to the Peruvian poet Manuel González Prada, the villanelle is a composition of rhymed three-lined stanzas starting with a double refrain that will alternate in the stanzas. Renaissance Italian in origin (page 28).

ZÉJEL   A Spanish poetic form believed to be of Arabic origin (10th – 11th centuries). It begins with a couplet, the first line of which becomes a refrain. Then follow two or three monorhymed tercets with different rhymes in each. At the end is a couplet, the last line of which is the refrain (page 110).

"ZEJELINE"   Derived from the Spanish-Arabic form of the Zéjel (10th and 11th centuries) at the "Living Poetry Research Seminar" in Catalonia, with an introductory couplet the first line of which becomes a refrain that is repeated with each new couplet. These alternate with tercets. The suffix "ine" indicates the rhyming scheme (page 17).

For Marcel·lí Alzina i Company,
my father,
architect of my life

Guida

For Joan, Mireia and Marc

Consol

GÜELL PARK

lok is a white dove, with beautiful wings and feathers. Every day he cleans them with his beak leaving them bright and shiny and ready to fly very high.

Flok is a traveller or, in other words, a messenger dove and he lives beyond the shores of our country. He is also a poet dove.

He loves going from place to place and finding out about everything. Travelling is his essential mission and he is very happy to fulfil it because, when people see him arriving at their dovecotes, they greet him at once, remove the message that he bears carefully tied to his leg, and then treat him really well until he has to return to his own country.

He enjoys flying near the sea, across the fields and through the squares of the cities and the towns. He likes the city especially and loves to fly up onto the rooftops and lamp-posts, to stretch his wings in the streets, to drink at the fountains . . . and, when it is appropriate and he feels inspired, to compose the rhymes of a poem.

Flok is happy today because he is bringing a message from far away and he'll be going through Barcelona, a city which is more or less close to the place where he has to take the message. He can already make out the old city and, since he is tired after all his flying, he decides to rest there for a little while.

He looks down and . . .

"What's that shining down there among the trees?"
He glides down to the ground.
"What on earth does that say?"
If Flok could read as well as he composes verses, he would know that it says "Güell Park".
"What crooked walls! What a strange shape they have. They're almost..."

Güell Park: *the entrance pavilion.*

This is a very curvy boat
and a cross not a flag it flies;
through its portholes it takes note
of the sea of time it plies
from its anchorage onshore where it must float.

Poetic form: Quintet

After composing the poem – which demonstrates that Flok might well be the first truly winged poet – he flies over the fence at the entrance.
"Goodness, that was a long haul!"
Once again he is seized by the gremlin of inspiration:

This stairway climbs and climbs up ever so high
and the cave at the top has a shady bench to try.

There's a medallion on the stairs halfway up the mountain
with a strange head whose mouth there acts as a fountain.

Its water trickles down to the flowers from a little pool
and smiling they bloom as they wash in its bath so cool.

Poetic form: Couplets

Güell Park: *Main stairway*

Flok suddenly sees something very surprising:
"What's that I see? It's a dragon! Lucky it's not doing much ... Maybe it's asleep ..."
And once again he comes out with a poem:

Güell Park: *the dragon*

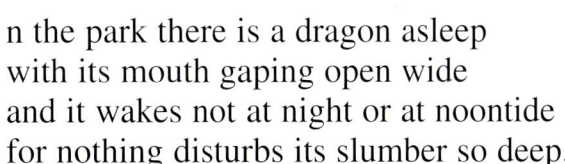n the park there is a dragon asleep
with its mouth gaping open wide
and it wakes not at night or at noontide
for nothing disturbs its slumber so deep.

All the colours adorn its body in bliss
and when the sun sends its light in showers,
thinking it is a mass of flowers,
a butterfly comes to leave it a kiss.

Poetic form: Rhyming "envelope" quatrain (abba)

Güell Park: *Doric colonnade*

Just in case the dragon awakes, Flok flies up to the columned amphitheatre.
He can't fly around here, but curiosity makes him walk inside.
"Wow! It's so deep! I feel so small in here! It's like coming into the land of the sun . . .
The brightness once again kindles his poetic flame:

Like a dream covered over in tiles,
the wide space is embroidered in light,
high the columns rise alone in their aisles
to the sun that is cloudless and bright.

Poetic form: Greek feet: Anapaests

Feeling a little dizzy from looking up so much, Flok wants to rest a little and he starts looking for a quiet place.
He sees a square and immediately flies over to it.
"That's a fine choice I've made! I've landed right in the middle of a snake. And it's so long . . .!"
Flok sits there thinking for a while . . .

Güell Park: *the bench that surrounds the square*

snake is guarding the whole square,
sees all but devours nothing there.
    He forms a seat
that also covers his flank complete.
    Right there he stays
for if he moves his fine skin will graze.
    Yet he has feet
like a lion's but with no path to complete.
    He shines so bright
dazzling sun and wind with his light.

Poetic form: the Catalan "Codolada"

After a little rest, Flok feels hungry and he looks around to see if he can find a few crumbs to eat.
An avenue of palm trees catches his eye and he flies up to have a look at them.
"I thought that palm trees were plants but . . . here they are made of stone . . . yet the ones over there are real!
What a very strange thing!"
Poor Flok is quite confused and tries to work it out . . . In verse, of course!

There are palm trees along the way
some of them real and some of them not,
a little mixed together in their display . . .

With ropes of hard rock they take root
and through summer and winter they stand
but forever unripe will be their fruit.

A date has fallen from one of the palms.
The fruit is surely real!
And this plant is too with all nature's charms.

Poetic form: Stornello

Güell Park: *Retaining wall.*

Flok flies into the air a couple of times to stretch his wings.
He sees a pine grove and a lot of trees. He thinks that there can be no more surprises left for him but as he flies closer he is entranced once again...
"These things are pin cushions and they're made of stone!
But... now they look like balconies!

Güell Park:
Avenue of tree columns

There between earth and sky
the balustrade is a veil that might fly

as fine as silk that brushes by
or maybe the web the spider weaves
and when the sun shines one believes

that it is honey to the eye
there between earth and sky.

When afternoon sinks through the leaves
the burning horizon filters through
to light with calm the day with its hue

or when evening comes and the day relieves
it cradles the rocks and roots up high

there between earth and sky.

Poetic form: "Zejeline" (neologism)

Our little friend Flok isn't sure where to go next because everything he sees seems to be magic and enchanted. He has never seen anything like this before and everything surprises him.
But what's happening now?
He's turning his head as if he can't fly straight . . .
"Oh dear, I don't know what's the matter. I can't tell if I'm flying crooked or if the walls are crooked and they're going to fall on me . . ."
Flok lands on the wall to try to stop his head from spinning and, now that his wings are still, it is his imagination that starts to fly.

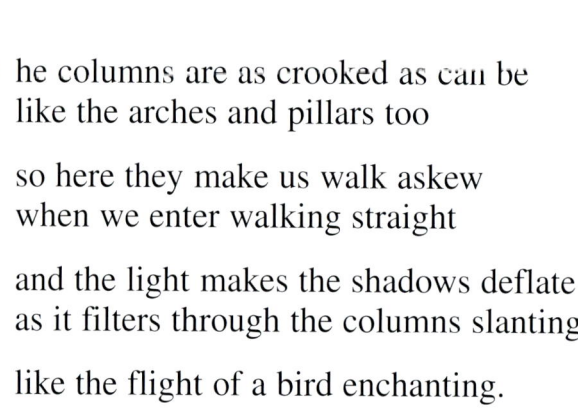

The columns are as crooked as can be
like the arches and pillars too

so here they make us walk askew
when we enter walking straight

and the light makes the shadows deflate
as it filters through the columns slanting

like the flight of a bird enchanting.

Poetic form: "Distine" (neologism)

Güell Park: *Curved portico-viaduct*

Somewhat baffled, Flok flies out and . . . is surprised to find a lady.
He thinks . . .
"What on earth is she doing here, standing so still and straight?
Maybe she's doing the same as me and has come out for a breath of fresh air."
But the lady isn't breathing or moving.
Then Flok realises that she's only a statue and he devotes his muse to her . . .

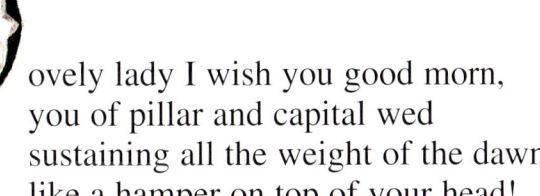

ovely lady I wish you good morn,
you of pillar and capital wed
sustaining all the weight of the dawn
like a hamper on top of your head!

Poetic form: Epigram

Güell Park: *Washerwoman column.*

Pleased with his epigram, Flok flies up to the mountaintop.
"What a lot of forest and what a wonderful view!"
Seeking the best vantage point, he lands on the highest point of the Three Crosses.
"It's fantastic!"
A beautiful poem blooms in Flok like a bouquet of emotions . . .

Güell Park: *the Three Crosses*

What a view I can see from up here,
the total extension of light!
The city is huge and nestled so near
and the horizon hugs the sea tight.

On top of the cross that has most height,
above the green and leafy frontier,
in my wings I still feel the flight,
its magic and emotion very dear.

I have seen how the hard stone flowered
and a forest completely bedecked:
with a thousand colours it was showered.

The wind brings me voices to select
and with its poetry I am empowered
on this peak where Three Crosses stand erect.

Poetic form: Sonnet

BELLESGUARD

As if in a dream and really moved by what he has seen, Flok does not know what he's flying over or where he's going. He flies and flies, up to the top part of the city. He sees a high point in the form of a cross, like or similar to the one he has left behind . . .
"What a perfect lookout! It's a wonderful view from up here . . ."
And Flok, being so curious by nature, admires the sight . . . and thinks:

The cloud just listens
at the sight of such beauty
silently rising.

Poetic form: Haiku.

Bellesguard: *Main facade*

Flok walks in the garden pecking at crumbs among the pebbles.
Tiles, in all the colours of the rainbow, catch his eye.
"Goodness! What a strange seat that is . . .
It must have been a lot of work to do such big designs with such small stones . . .
It looks as if it's leaning against the façade . . ."

Bellesguard:
seat at the main entrance

T he bench against the façade leaning
is unmoving, absent and indifferent
and for it filigree has no meaning . . .

The grandeur it will never understand
is from artist's hands that modelled its form
humble and simple but the creation is grand.

Dressed in a thousand and one colours bright
it rests in the sovereign shadow screening
of the tall cross that contemplates day and night

the bench against the façade leaning.

Poetic form: Madrigal

Flok is once again on his way but, as he flies off, he looks back at the top of the castle...

ike a castle under a spell
it raises its head in the air
to view the immensity well.

The chimney pierces with its shell
the blue sky or storm looming there,
like a castle under a spell.

Each battlement, a sentinel,
from the roof edge all of them stare
to view the immensity well.

The spirit captures us too in its snare
like a castle under a spell
to view the immensity well.

Poetic form: Villanelle

Bellesguard: *Detail of one of the towers*

TERESIAN COLLEGE

"And still more crosses!" . . . Flok thinks.
So of course . . . he stops again.

Teresian College: *Battlements and corner of the building*
Detail of the lock on one of the doors

At every chamfer is a cross
by bold battlements surrounded
and their tips rise up into the sky
creating infinity's crown.
Unyielding Teresian fortress
with stones lit by light divine
"that die because they do not die"
but forever live on in the heart.

Poetic form: Blank verse

Teresian College:
Detail of the ironwork at the main gate

There's no stopping Flok who goes from one side to the other of the garden, not missing a thing . . .
"It would have been terrible if I hadn't seen this . . .!"
An ironwork gate obliges him fly up . . . and he thinks:

he iron exploded into a gate
a grille there to procreate.

This is a truly wonderful thing
the entrance and doorway barring
and like a sentinel of the king,
ductile metal forges this grate.

All this ironwork is a sign:
two hearts in faithful love entwine,
that of Carmel, of the star divine
and the hill of the cross and Christ's fate.

Threads in woven harmony here stay
looking out to the light of day
and filtering the fantastic play
of the iron exploded into a gate.

Poetic form: Tristich with cauda

He is so absorbed in his investigations that he doesn't notice he's entered a gallery.
"Now I don't know where I am or if I'll be able to get out of here."
As he peers through the windows he admires . . .

atiny light and glowing shade
in a rainbow cavalcade.

Arches soar like candlelight
reflecting motes of lily white
in a rainbow cavalcade.

The portal's calm of glowing peace
ensures that beauty must increase
in a rainbow cavalcade.

Poetic form: Song with parallelism Provençal style

Teresian College:
Arched gallery

Leaving the astonishing college, Flok flies over the city and hovers around four houses that have also attracted him with their beauty and distinction . . .
It doesn't take long for the poems to come into his mind. Each house has its own rhythm and art, from foundations to rooftop.

VICENS

MILÀ

THE HOUSES

BATLLÓ

CALVET

Casa Vicens: *Cornice and gallery*

CASA VICENS

Explosion not stopping for anything
here in the city centre ascending,

    a day in Spring
blooming with a thousand tiles:

    flowers with smiles
raising their heads in bold display

    catch light of day.
When the sun shines its splendid light

It dazzles us like perfume bright.

Poetic form: "Codolina" (neologism)

Lamps on the cast-iron fence

here are two troubadours of light
keeping watch here at the gate
and balconies dressed with flowers
where maybe two fairies lie sleeping.

There are two troubadours of light
that shine bright at the end of day
over the iron grapevine leaves
and the palm-tree balcony's grace.

The two troubadours of light
sing and sing the whole night through
weaving their silent verses

to shed light on the building's face.
The two troubadours of light
go out to make way for the light of day.

Poetic form: English morpho-sonnet (or ballad)

CASA MILÀ
(OR LA PEDRERA - "THE QUARRY

Casa Milà – (*La Pedrera* – "The Quarry")
Detail of the rooftop

n army of stone from its silent domain,
heroic and noble flames watch each in place
impassively bearing the wind and the rain.

Olympian gods or warriors asleep,
sublime in their sculpture and unrevealed face,
they are silent and kingly in the night watch they keep.

Poetic form: Greek feet (amphibrachs)

Casa Milà ("*La Pedrera*" or "The Quarry")
Detail of the facade

Sea of rock crashes on the building's face
beating the rugged and deep precipice endless.
Stone under spell of long quiet pulsing waves
    - hymn the foam sings -.

Rebels the waves beating the rock in vain
forming a thousand coves of vital space
silent sonata of arpeggios mute:
    - hymn the foam sings -.

Poetic form: Sapphic ode

CASA BATLLÓ

Th e city's party dress is abloom
with all the golden hues of broom,
in many tones captivated
and mystery and disguise created.

Each balcony wears a mask the while
to cover up its mocking smile …
thinking, as ever upwards they peer,
that carnival is always here.

Poetic form: Quatrain with caudate rhyme

Casa Batlló: *Detail of the façade*

ay up on the roof above
sleeps a dragon of form divine
and fitting him almost like a glove
he wears a rosary on his spine.

Fine as silk is one side of him
the other of silver scales;
between them a streamer is the trim
crowned by the wind and its gales.

Poetic form: Quatrain (abab)

Casa Batlló: *Detail of the attic ridge*

Casa Calvet
Doorknocker

CASA CALVET

The doorknocker must be struck
and if we have a little luck
we'll stun or perhaps do worse
to the bug fixed here under a curse
forever imprisoned with each shock
that comes with every cast-iron knock.

Every blow attempts to kill,
and thus the knocker's aim fulfil,
the incarnation of all that is bad
and with every blow that it has had
the bug seems fused ever more
to the iron on the entrance door.

Poetic form: Sexain

he loud voice calling is not hoarse.
What is begun is not yet ended.
A Solomonic column rises with force
like a long ringlet well attended.

Poetic form: Malaysian pantun

Casa Calvet: *Detail of the balusters, lift buttons, and Solomonic column at the entrance*

"Maybe I've spent too much time here, but … oh, it was certainly worth having a look at …!"
It sees that this idea is very familiar to Flok because, talking about having a look, he stops short in front of the huge entrance to Güell Palace.

GÜELL PALACE

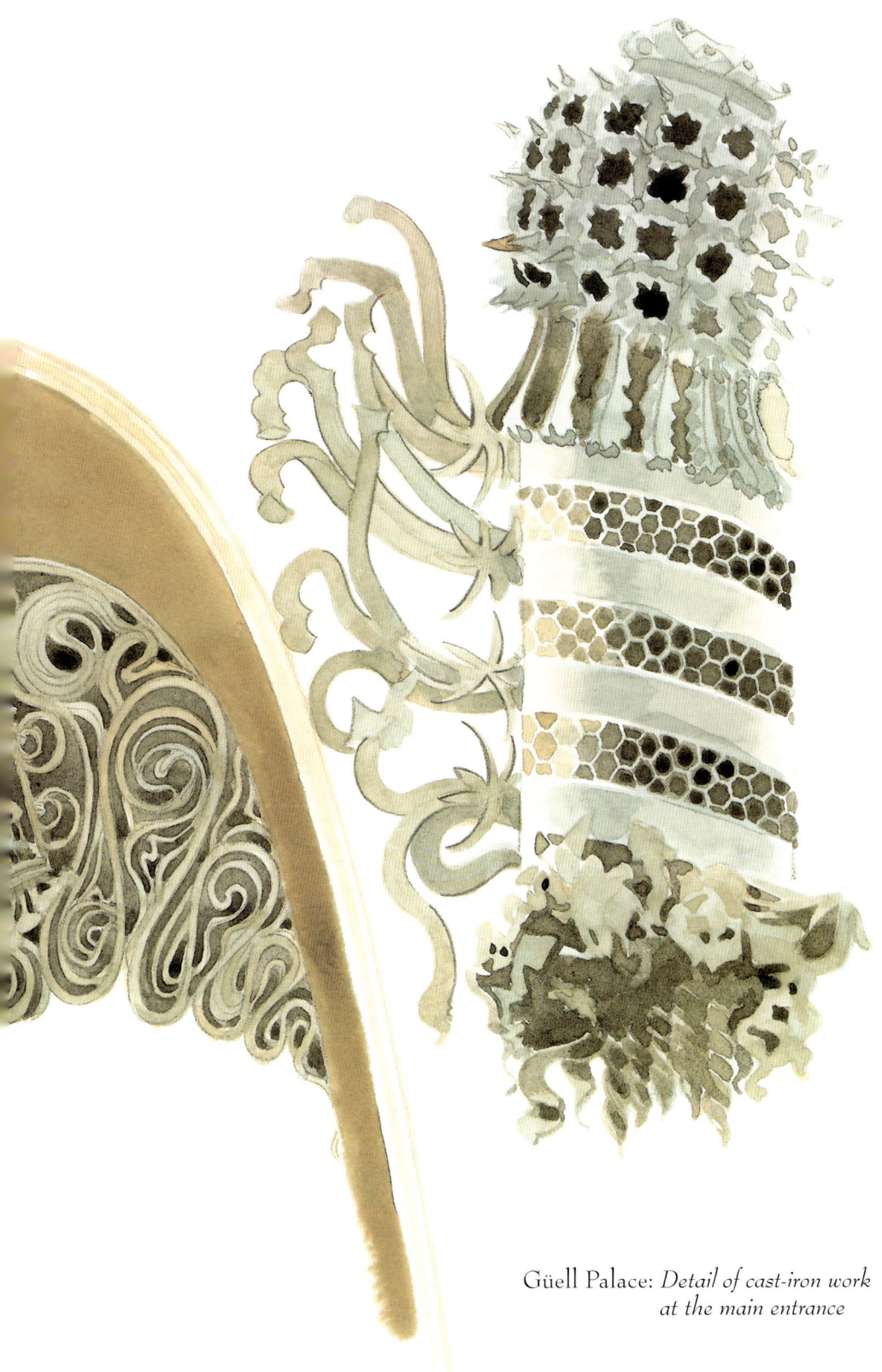

Güell Palace: *Detail of cast-iron work at the main entrance*

In a flurry of wings he goes up to the roof terrace.
"I would never have imagined that trees would grow up on a roof terrace.... Or are they trees?
I don't know if they're chimneys or brightly coloured plants ..."

igh on this roof a garden has been made
where plants their fantasy colours parade
with the luxuriant foliage of the trees
knowing that their leaves will not die or fade.

Chisel and hammer hewed roots on high
with caramel-hued bark to beautify
while flashing gems their colours so bright
embellish the trunk that climbs to the sky.

Poetic form: Persian or Omar Khayyám quatrain

Güell Palace
Detail of chimneys on the roof terrace

Street Lamps in the Plaça Reial and Pla de Palau

LAMP-POST

Our little friend Flok leaves the rooftops and footpaths. It's nearly dark and he decides to go and sleep somewhere. He is guided by some very singular lights.
"I feel as if I was right in the middle of the stars.
Oh, what a beautiful light!"

ight here in the square some stars are born,
their luminous pool lights tranquil night,
a space of longing they adorn
and climb to the sky, a kiss of light.

Their arms are long in artistic play
and scatter silken silver in beams.
Each one is fire sent out in a ray
to light the night with all its gleams.

Poetic form: Greek feet – iambic meter

Flok likes the street lamps so much that he has flown up higher, to hover around the area trying to see if there are any more …
"It looks as if there are some glow-worms down there winking at me. Goodness, what strange street lamps they are, and they're wearing a hat!"
The light of the muse is lit in Flok …

Rising from amid the shadows and silence
a helmeted column would kiss the moon,
discrete and white with tones of maroon,
high above the radiant globes of light.
Glow-worms they seem in their vigil in the dark,
blinking and twinkling their eyes at night's star,
sending showers of light to infinity afar
pulsing through the smooth belly of night.

Poetic form: Italian octave

Lamp-posts: *Ciutadella Park*

The sound of water makes him feel thirsty and he flies over to a waterfall.
"This is beautiful! And … what can that be up there?"
Once again Flok's artistic inquisitiveness takes over. He can't resist going over to see what it is …

ight at the top, behind the waterfall,
it resides, sad memory lost and old;
time's ravages have the doorway in thrall
but death has not robbed the charm of this threshold.
When the sun has shone through the arcades all
the stone is lit in rays of flame and gold
embellishing the lizard lazing there
mid-medallion, yawning prisoner in his lair.

Poetic form: Royal octave

Aquarium: *Ciutadella Park*

Flok flies on a little further. The park gardens, the lawns everywhere and well-tended plants are very soothing. He feels good here.
In a series of little hops and short flights, he approaches a kind of balustrade surrounding a statue of the poet Aribau.
Flok is more impressed with the balustrade, which is full of figures and relief work, than with the statue itself.
Then Flok imitates Aribau:

light has stopped short at the stone
with homage amid the green
in the stone balustrade screen
circling the figure here alone.
From the heights where they have grown
trees shade the lions in their beds
resting their drowsy heads
and by the slight chill of shadows kissed
when through the fresh morning mist
the sun heats the cool that night spreads.

Poetic form: Décima or espinella

THE ARIBAU BALUSTRADE

Detail of the balustrade:
Ciutadella Park

From the bust of Aribau, and attracted by the salty fragrance of the sea, Flok flies off towards the port.
And, hardly aware of what he is doing, he perches on a kind of gently-rocking rail.
This regular movement soon lulls Flok off to sleep.
He is awakened by the early morning light and is surprised to find himself at sea. He takes off to stretch his wings and, high in the air, he can make out the graceful silhouette of land in the midst of the blue sea. Ever-curious, he goes to have a look.
He has reached the port, but it's not the one where he went to sleep. Then his artist's gaze is caught by a majestic temple …

Palma de Mallorca: *Cathedral*

CATHEDRAL
PALMA DE MALLORCA

The grandest windows like the temple's eyes
look out with irises of a thousand hues
and the sun laughs at them when their gaze he spies.

Poetic form: Terzina with fourth paeons

As if by magic and not knowing which way he's come or how he got there, Flok now finds himself flying among the pines in this surprising garden.
"I feel like I'm inside a story! It's so wonderful, everything I can see here …"

La Pobla de Lillet:
Archway in the "Can Artigues" (Artigues House) garden

"CAN ARTIGUES" (Artigues House)
OR "THE MAGNESIUM FOUNTAIN"

The rockeries welcome me here where I've flown
tracing their arches to decorate the way,
strong arms entwined and made of rugged stone,
dancing hoops opening the garden where I'll stay.
Through the pines a group of monumental doors
hide spellbound fables of love and wars,
of fairies or genies in old legends and lores
that flowered in the light of an earlier day.

Poetic form: Lyrical octave

"I must go. If I stay here looking at everything I'll never leave!"
And as Flok flies off, he keeps looking back to admire what he's left behind.

In nature's glory   here in all the green,
atop this mountain   of stones dressed in grey,
around the tower   the wind has its way
under a pure sky   in light aquamarine.
Idyllic landscape   all around this scene
with its silent path   in the starry night,
in fragrance of buds   greets first morning light
while the air pours out   draughts of day serene.

Poetic form: Cobla (arte mayor)

La Pobla de Lillet: *Tower in the "Can Artigues" gardens*

ied to my leg is the note I must bear
and I must set out on this task of mine
but I have seen all this scenery so fair
and works of art so rare and divine

that have captivated my wings
as I've followed their path of light …
Mystery of breathing art it brings
sending its perfume to my flight!

With this note tied to my leg I came
and I shall fly high with a flourish
but memories of this will be the flame
that my tomorrow will nourish.

Still I must travel far through the air
So that I might deliver the message I bear.

Poetic form: Shakespearian sonnet

Flok returns to Barcelona …
"Goodness, what a huge city this is!
But I think it's the one I already flew over where I saw such amazing things. Though … I didn't think I saw those strange fingers sticking up into the sky.
Let's go and have a closer look …

THE SAGRADA FAMILIA EXPIRATORY CHURCH

As he approaches, Flok sees that it is a tree full of other doves.
"Look at all those doves … I'm going over to say hullo!"

ranches in the wind, the stars and the sun
where through thick green leaves making its way
like buds a flight of birds has now begun
to make of the cypress a floral spray.

Where through thick green leaves making its way
a shoot of faith like a torch flames above
to make of a stone cypress a floral spray
symbol of eternal grandeur and love.

A shoot of faith like a torch flames above
to crown the treetop like a bouquet in the sky
symbol of eternal grandeur and love
like white wings that bear the doves as they fly.

Rising to heaven floats their silent song
to proclaim the marvels that God has done,
tall finger that sustains eternal and strong
branches in the wind, the stars and the sun.

Poetic form: French Pantun

Sagrada Familia expiatory church: *Detail of the cypress, Nativity façade*

There are so many things to attract Flok's attention that he flies a little higher to admire some motionless bubbles frothing from the tips of the "fingers".
And from Flok a poem bubbles forth.

Bubbles of stone are adorning this spire,
a rosary of pearls strung by faith evergreen,
or, wet by the rains, buttons of sun-fire
shed drops of light's breath with delicate sheen.
Flaming waves under a sky serene.

Poetic form: Quintain

Sagrada Familia expiatory church:
Tip of the spire on the Nativity facade

Needing to rest a while, Flok perches on a windowsill and contemplates the spires. "From over there it was like bubbles, but from here I can see a star!"

An open window is the guard here alone
where between a patch of sky and infinity wide
the star of purple and gold high has flown
rising to kiss the moon, midnight's bride
or patch over a little of the sun on its throne
and scrutinising space from side to side.
The window is open gazing wide-eyed
where it has framed woven light and stone.

Poetic form: Classical octave

Sagrada Familia expiatory church:
Detail of the spire on the Nativity façade seen from the atrium

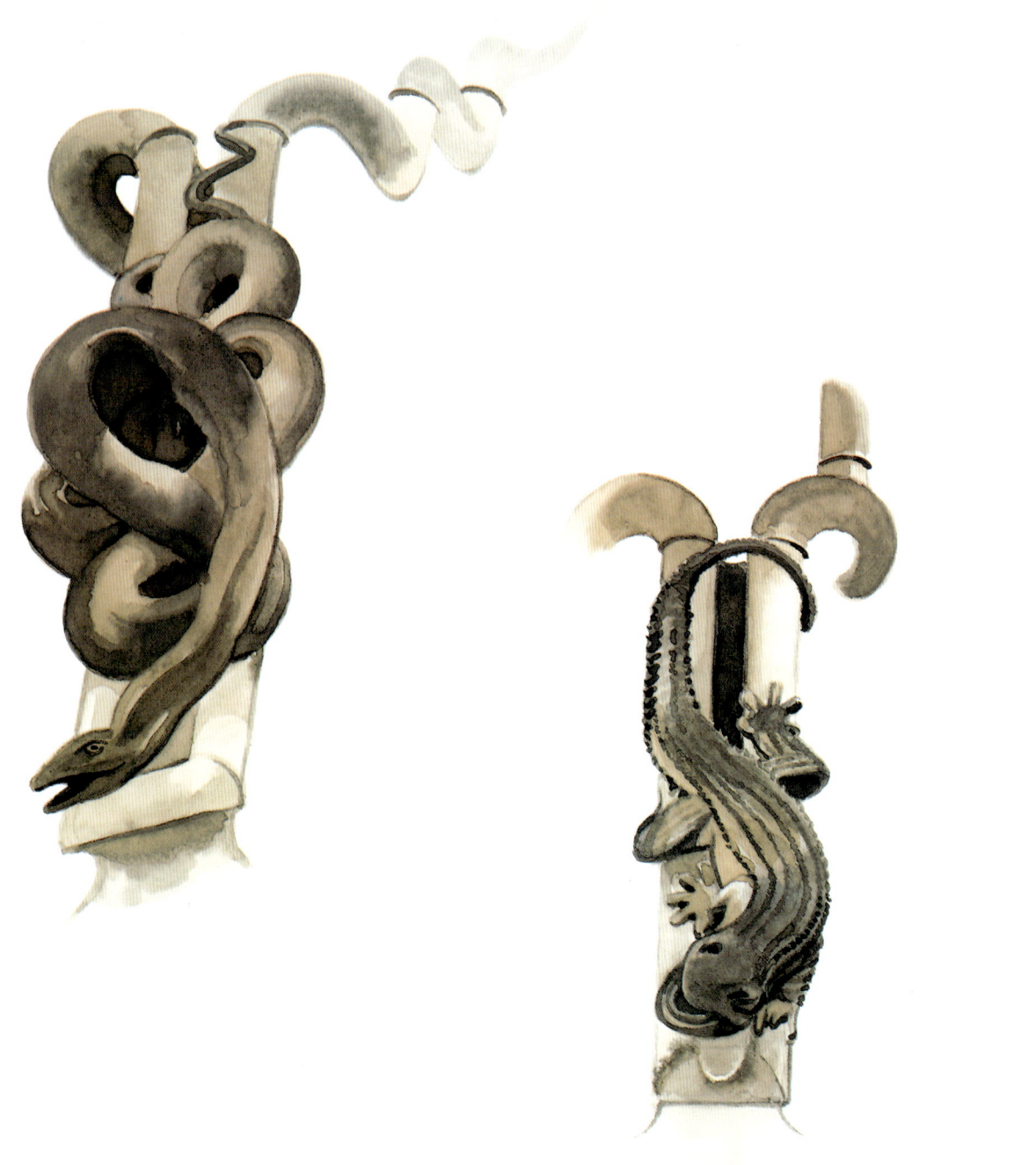

DETAIL OF GARGOYLES AND BASE OF A COLUMN

"I really must go, but I want to fly once more around this magic forest of high spires …"

Higher and higher right up to the sky!
Like eight arms reaching out to the dawn
they embrace the intangible early morn
and caress the cheek of a star on high.

Higher and higher right up to the sky!
Like shining arrows the evening they adorn
and as they rise up the grey clouds are torn
and the dark cover made by night's dye.

Spires that are steeped in clarity and light
are seen the horizon round all day and night;
the stonemason's art is their beautifier.

Sculptures of stone ropes intertwined,
filigree work like lace refined
with a lace-maker's plait as unifier.

Higher and higher!
To seven-veiled astral bareness fly,
higher and higher up to the sky!

Poetic form: Sonnet with estrambote

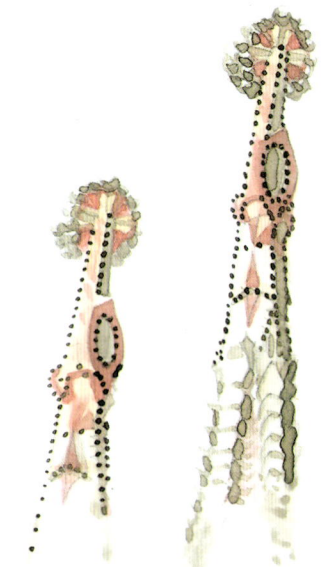

Sagrada Familia expiatory church: *Detail of the spires*

"But this is very strange! What are these waves doing in the middle of the city?"
Once again Flok stops to have a look.

he waves that have come here to play
make castles of wind and sand;
unmoving and in their tones of grey
they cast shadows west through the land.

Ghostly fires of a stone sea they stay
a silent screen or a ceiling spanned
and children's laughter during the day
they muffle as if with a gentle hand.

Reddish waves with no sandy beach
stretching under the shadowy reach
of eight tall fingers signing the heights.

Heavy sea, sleepy and aloof
transformed into a soundless roof
where the stars come to sail through their nights.

Poetic form: Sonnet ("arte menor")

Sagrada Familia classrooms

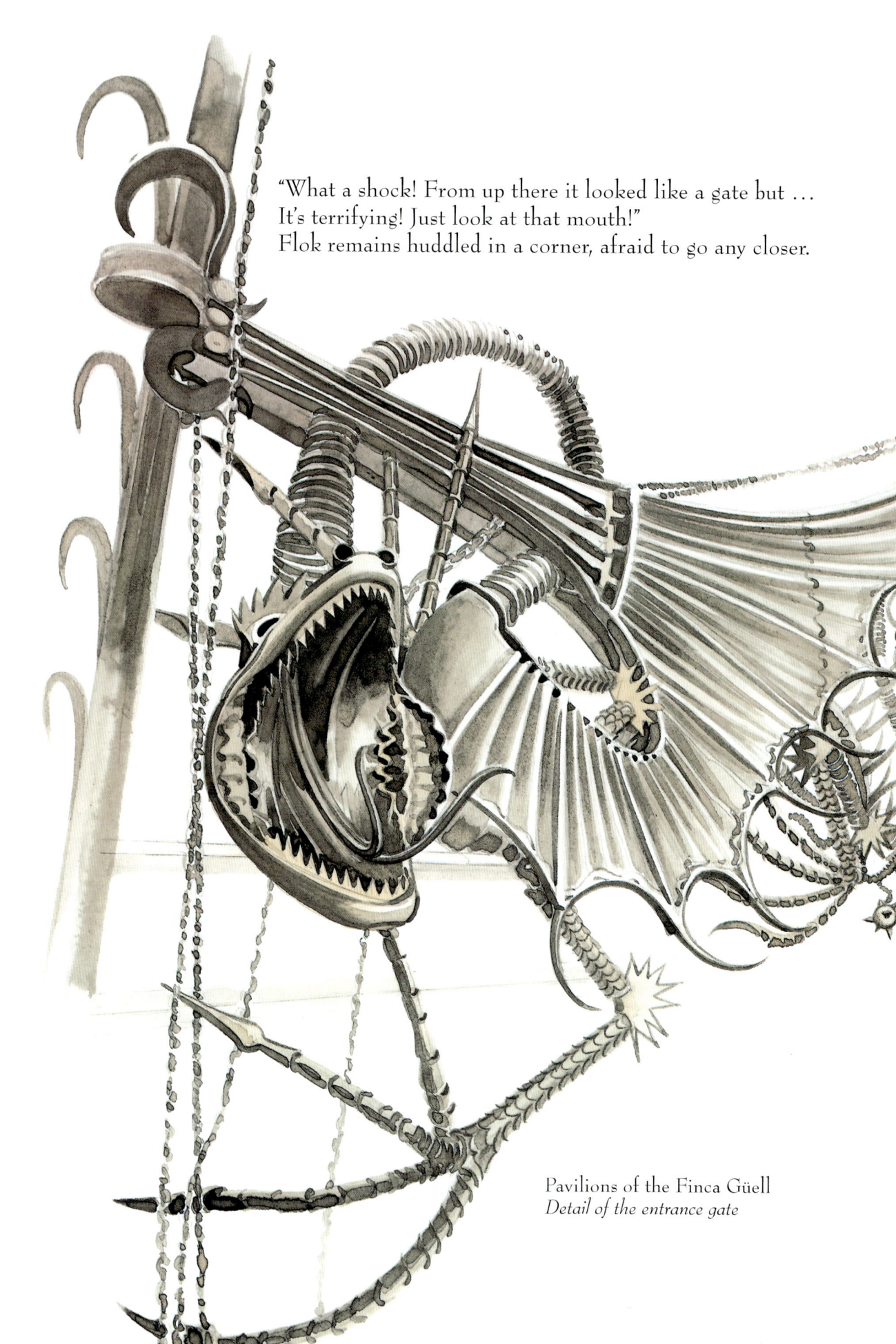

"What a shock! From up there it looked like a gate but …
It's terrifying! Just look at that mouth!"
Flok remains huddled in a corner, afraid to go any closer.

Pavilions of the Finca Güell
Detail of the entrance gate

PAVILIONS AT THE FINCA GÜELL

I am afraid of this very strange thing.
I am afraid of the head and each tooth terrifies.
I am afraid of the eyelashes here framing
its ferocious and powerful eyes
that burn right into the entrails they're claiming.

I am afraid of the claws for each horrifies.
I am afraid of these curled and twisted feet.
I am afraid of the strong nails that my eye spies
just like four long spears sharp and complete
about to flay the four winds in the skies …

He thinks he is lord of all of the nights,
and watches through darkness until the day clear
instilling fear in the heart and the eye that alights
thinks he will spit out the poison he keeps here
in his long tongue's lash and his terrible bites.

I am afraid of this dragon that I see so near.

Poetic form: "Quintine" (neologism)

Still very frightened, Flok leaves as fast as he can before the dragon can lash out and claw him. He flies up to a roof where he is distracted by something like a brightly-coloured flowerpot.
"Phew! What a relief to get away from that monster!"
Now that he has recovered from the fright, he flies around for a while.

rom afar they are cacti   kissing the sun
from afar their spiky points   scratch at the morn
and filling with bright brushstrokes   where blue is born
in the woolliness of clouds   soft and fine-spun.
Colours brilliant that dazzle   each tiny piece
colours of a fantasy bud   the sky adorn
in the bright garden forever   blooming in peace.

Poetic form: "Heptamera" (neologism)

Finca Güell
Detail of ventilators and light trap

Finca Güell: *Secondary gate*

Alone and yawning
is your oval mouth open
while voice still muted
encloses in its silence
auras unsighted.

Poetic form: Tanka

Finca Güell: *the Hercules Fountain*

With each drop falling
you deliver eternal
harmony's sweetness,
an embrace as you freshen
a font where the moon drowses.

Poetic form: Tanka

And Flok wonders …
"What on earth is that huge tortoise doing down there in the street …?"
He goes to have a look.
"But … it's an entrance!

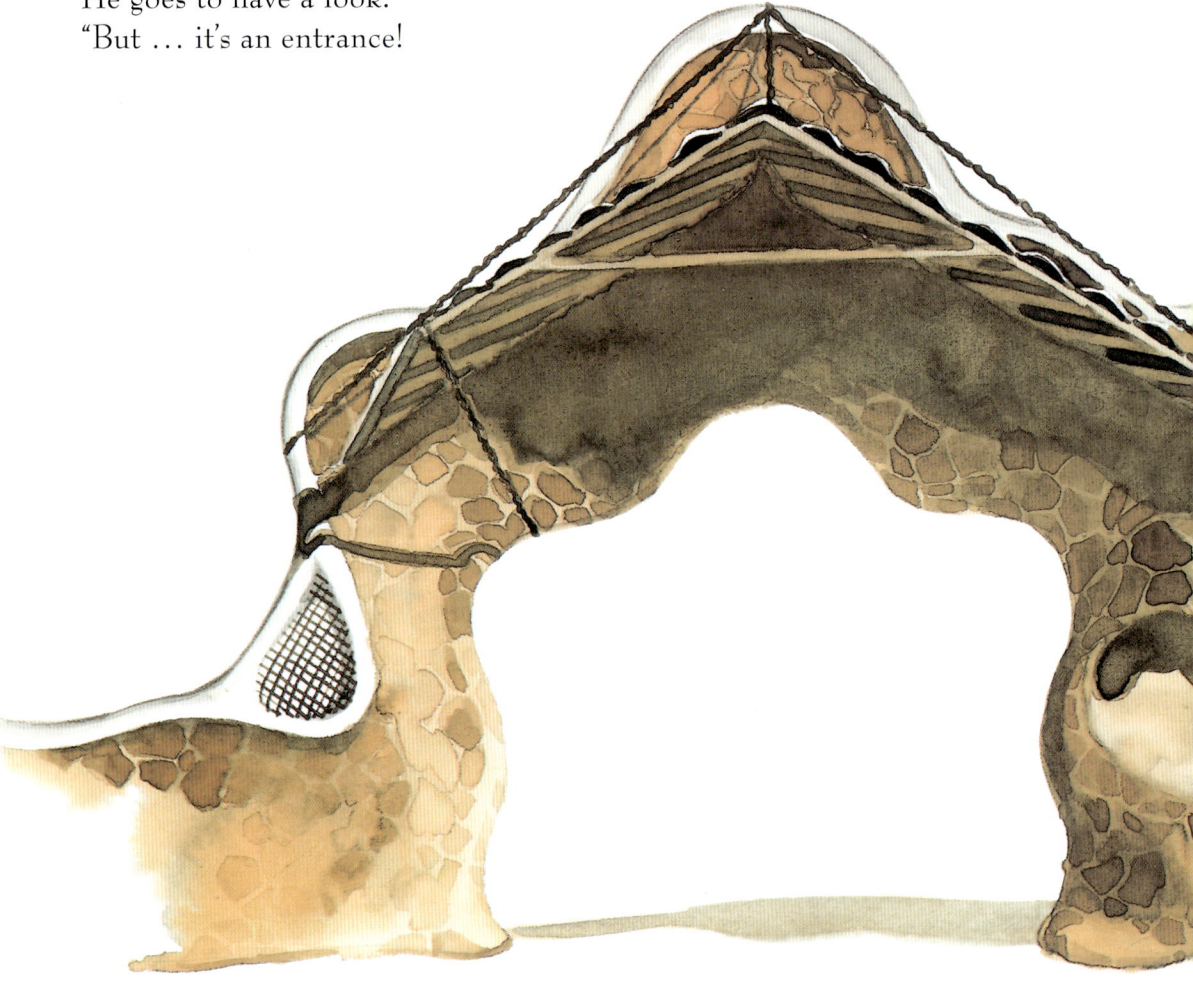

ENTRANCE TO THE FINCA MIRALLES

A giant tortoise bars the way
blocks it to nearly everyone
   and with its shell
   – sound as a bell –
it takes the rain and wind and sun.

All its belly is like a route
of form that's sinuous and fine
   and shrewd and proud
   barrier avowed
for those who try to cross the line.

Poetic form: Espluguesian stanza (named after its creator Josep Esplugues i Bator)

Tired of all the noise, people and cars, he flies away from the big city. Suddenly he sees a pine forest and decides to go down.
"How lovely it is and what beautifully contrasting light!"

 fine mesh of peace envelops the air
and arpeggios of light play on the stone,
while there in the shadow's cool all alone
an unperfumed flower hides out of the glare.

Amongst the pines and the green overgrown
there silently crouches an open door,
near the fingers of a hand like a bright meteor
guarding the portal and bright-hued art here shown.

The shadows and light give life evermore
while faith runs free with the lovely forms
in the artist's creations that here joyfully soar.

Each stone conserves his breath that warms
and the stained glass bright with the fire of his glance
creates a calm rainbow safe from all storms

and a sunset of prayers the dawn will enhance.

Poetic form: "Sonina" (neologism)

COLONIA GÜELL CRYPT

Colonia Güell crypt: *entrance door*

"Now I'm going to tell this butterfly what I've seen so far ...
It's so beautiful that it really deserves a special poem!"

The caterpillar in a ray of light through the window came
with wild fantasies crowding the clarity of its mind.
It wanted to wear the charm of the moon
and the beauty adorning the star,
take the blue from the sky
become a flower
of air.
Like ne'er,
tears fall this hour
and a tender song is his cry
with tears from a honey-toned reservoir;
sliding down his cheek and falling in festoon.
To embrace him like a mother comes the sun's breath kind
dressing him as a butterfly with wildflower wings' brightness aflame.

Poetic form: Altar poem

Colonia Güell crypt: *the stained glass "butterfly"*

Flok glides around so that he can have a good look down at a steep craggy mountain range.

mountain range explodes and reaches out
to touch an august and spellbound sky
a thousand fingers brushing eternity on high,
Holy Mystery fixed here for all the devout.

Light from above leaves a kiss like a sigh.
Glory and sky have become this hard rock
and a flash of love is architecture's shock
that has sculpted the four-barred shield nearby.

The sun's rays finding the fissure a block
pour golden motes over rocky stalagmite
to light the divine shadow here recondite
with its fire born when the heights unlock.

A living people's mountain, immortal light!

Poetic form: "Quartine" (neologism)

FIRST MYSTERY OF THE GLORY
MONTSERRAT

First Mystery of the Glory: *Montserrat*

GÜELL CELLARS
GARRAF

Flok flies on and on. His white wings break the blue of the sky and he becomes a moving point over the azure of the sea, almost as if he were playing among the waves and the sheer cliffs along the coast. He remembers that he must deliver the message and continues on his way, but from high in the sky he admires a kind of stone tent he can see crouched on the shore.

Near a beautiful camp of cool rock grey
the tent's like a sail unmoved by the breeze
and the waves of the sea have come to stay;
for stone winds hold it with ease and they weigh.

Poetic form: Omar Khayýam quatrain (with internal variation)

Flok is quite tired as he has flown a long way. But he is happy with what he has seen.
He decides to stop and rest a little. Not far ahead he can make out some very high towers. He tries to glide around them but then he finds something surprising …

"What's this? Are they big hats, or maybe they're nests?
I don't know if I can believe my eyes … but, yes, they're storks!
Now I know why I'm so tired. This means I've flown a very long way.
But where can I be now? Have I flown off my route?
But Flok has made no mistake. He's now reached the cathedral in León and he's on the right track.

Once he's recovered a little from his long flight and he's had a chat in his winged language with the storks, he flies down to the centre of a square in front of a building with very pointy towers.
"That's really beautiful!"

ith its four slender pointy hats
it's like a castle under a spell
rising so beautifully just here
in the city's heart a bright cell.
"Botines House" they tell me
is the name of this sentinel
a kind of toy in grey blocks of stone
its roof made in slate like a shell
and windows and still more windows
filtering golden light rays that swell
from the sun that shines in spring
and when winter snows come to dwell.

Poetic form: Ballad (arte menor)

Casa de los Botines: *main facade*

CASA DE LOS BOTINES
LEÓN

Casa de los Botines:
Doorway and ironwork entrance gate

Hippety-hop, Flok goes over to the main entrance …
"What a feeling of strength and security!"
As always, Flok's flights of thought and rhyme come together.

All of the entrance is like a huge wave
that makes its way inside
and always still on his crest rising brave,
sentry of the sun and the starry nave,
Saint George this house astride
watches the gate of the entrance so grave:
with coat of mail and blazons he imposes
and the nine stone steps he closes.

Poetic form: Silva

Casa de los Botines:
iron grille

Flok doesn't have much time for amusement, but everything he sees delights him and he responds in the best possible way …
"This grille goes on and on! It's got figures in it and spikes and it makes shadows everywhere. It's such beautiful filigree!"

A GRILLE OF IRON

Great rhythm surging from hammer blows.

Rich space in the wind where the thrust chopped.

Image so noble in fine work glows.

Like a shout of pride in the stone stopped.

Lithe spirit that in pure metal finds its repose.

Every twist is given its figure to adopt.

Only you are the gate that in the stone grows;

Filter of light with wonders you are topped.

In these walls made by craft of human hands,

Rhyming in clear spaces a thousand stars rejoice.

Or a cluster of lovely forms entwined here stands.

Nothingness was filled when the artist gave you voice.

Poetic form: Acrostic

Our little friend has been flying slowly around the corners of the building until he finally stops in amazement in front of one of the towers.
"Here's the perfect place for me to have a good rest and even sleep for a while!"
Maybe this vision of the dovecotes fills him with nostalgia for he left home days ago and he responds with a homesick verse ...

ike a pointed hat with a very sharp tip
its roof is like a coal-black strip.

A tower that is beautifully round
is a finger that has been crowned
by clouds drifting low near the ground,

and it climbs up high the daylight to rip
this pointed hat with a very sharp tip.

Four little houses each one a cell
are hung right here for me to dwell
with other doves I know very well

for they too fly to the horizon's lip
from this pointed hat with a very sharp tip.

Poetic form: Zéjel

Casa de los Botines: *north tower*

Flok is flying quietly around when he sees some jackdaws coming near.
They fly in front of him and point with their black wings to something not very far away.
"What do they want?
I think I'll follow them because they might want to show me something interesting …"
Flok flies behind them…

ow it is time to say goodbye
and fly away from León's sky,
enter Maragatería
where art has woven an idea
like sonatas spun in the air
to construct a great castle there,
dazzling as far as the eye can see
filling the plain like filigree
or a tapestry that seems to soar
from an Episcopal palace door.

Poetic form: "Decàmera" (neologism)

EPISCOPAL PALACE
ASTORGA

Episcopal Palace: *entrance*

Flok folds his wings and begins to walk around having a leisurely look. "What good luck that those jackdaws brought me here. This palace is really beautiful!"

The entrance has been nobly crowned,
with tassels and biretta designed.
This wood exploding from the ground

is beauty totally refined.
The stones of this Palace mute and hard
tell of a grandeur that is combined

with all the peace that they do guard!

Poetic form: Classical terzina

Episcopal Palace: *Main entrance*

With shining eyes he investigates every corner.
He knows he should move on but he can't leave until he has seen absolutely everything …
"The more I look, the more wonderful things I see …"
Flok continues to seek beauty, verse by verse …

f you walk around the Palace you'll find a door
tucked around a corner and easy to ignore,
and a narrow passage of stone from days of yore
hides an entrance with a knocker, one small door more.

Windows like toys you'll discover on the way
with sibylline grilles looking out to greet the day,
like branches about to flower in a spray
when you look at this corner from the garden so gay.

Poetic form: Monorhymed quatrain "cuaderna vía"

Episcopal palace: *bridge and entrance from the west wing of the apse.*

Flok reaches a point where the whole horizon is of an intense blue.
He thinks he is lost and doesn't know where to go.
Then he sees a seagull and flies over to ask him the way.

EL CAPRICHO
COMILLAS - SANTANDER

Flok follows the seagull's wise advice and is soon back on the right track again. It seems as if he has just about reached the end of his journey but ... he is distracted by a huge bunch of sunflowers.

caprice of sunflowers that together have flocked
to form a golden bunch and softly flowing mane
extends across Spring's green and lovely plain
as if in a cradle rocked
by the invisible hand of a cooling breeze.
A caprice that sparkles a brilliant green tune
of satin arpeggios over the trees
as if from a piano's keys
sings its sonata to the landscape here hewn.

Poetic form: Nine-line stanza or strophe

Flok goes around the house and stops to look at a balcony that juts from a corner.
"It's incredible to see flowers that seem to be blooming from the wall…"
And he continues his poetic work…

El Capricho: *Detail of a chamfer.*

I

Place of tranquil repose
with melancholy ease
in solitude to doze
in twilight harmonies.

A quiet bench does disclose
that in this refuge joy frees
a lovers' nook that glows
lit by far sky-blue seas.

The stone a garden has made
harvest of yellow and green
the pilgrim's wealth overlaid.

In tufts of lovely sheen
a sweet breeze comes to parade
while shadows play between.

II

In the calm afternoon
the balcony facing the wind
hearing the west wind's tune
has an iron seat here pinned.

In night's watch from the moon
a promise and oath twinned
with a peaceful dream's tune
and by feeling's arch disciplined.

And here it is Spring all year
borne by the air apace
around this balcony here.

Light drizzles through the space
to fill the place with cheer
giving dream its waking grace.

III

lace of tranquil repose in the calm afternoon
with melancholy ease the balcony facing the wind
in solitude to doze hearing the west wind's tune
in twilight harmonies has an iron seat here pinned.

A quiet bench does disclose in night's watch from the moon
that in this refuge joy frees a promise and oath twinned
a lovers' nook that glows with a peaceful dream's tune
lit by far sky-blue seas and by feeling's arch disciplined.

The stone a garden has made and here it is Spring all year,
harvest of yellow and green borne by the air apace,
the pilgrim's wealth overlaid around this balcony here.

In tufts of lovely sheen light drizzles through the space,
a sweet breeze comes to parade to fill the place with cheer
while shadows play between giving dream its waking grace.

Poetic form: Tri-sonnet (neologism)

Our little friend FLOK – for we can certainly say that he is our friend now – has reached his destination: a dovecote facing the sea has been ready and waiting for him for several days now.
Without a moment's hesitation he enters the little door and waits patiently while they take his message.
Gentle hands caress him and swiftly untie the small capsule attached to his leg.
He is satisfied. Maybe he has dawdled a little but … now he has completed his task of bearing and delivering the message.
It would be going too far to say that he has stopped being inquisitive, because this is not the case. FLOK is very curious to know what important matter has made him fly so far so he listens attentively trying to find out what is in the message.

A surprised voice exclaims:
"Look, it's from those friends we met in Barcelona! It says …"

> *Following your advice, we have visited Gaudí's works.*
> *We are all impressed by the whole itinerary and by the personality of this great architect. We will never be able o express our gratitude enough for all the addresses, routes and information you gave us. We hope to return to your country again next year and that we will see each other again.*
>
> *With best wishes,*
> *The KOLF family*

FLOK is amazed to hear what the letter says.
It seems that, without knowing it, he has brought from his country an expression of gratitude for the writer's discovery of the incomparable art of a man named GAUDÍ, the very one who has both caused him to arrive late and stimulated his poetic muse.

With enormous curiosity, he listens in to the conversation between the people who are up on the roof terrace.

It is a vivid discussion, with questions from those who know less and answers from those who know more about the subject, that enlivens the calm afternoon ...

So, Antoni Gaudí was an architect?

Yes and, in particular, his profession was not just a way of earning a living but "life itself" for him.

HE SAID:
> *Architecture, for me, is my way of expressing myself, my very way of being. I seek beauty, and beauty is the splendour of truth, and to discover the truth one needs to make a very profound study of creation. An artist's mission is to create beauty and beauty is life, life in movement that culminates in man.*

Does that mean that Gaudí's art was full of fantasy?

No, not in the least.

> *Fantasy is something irrational, a kind of delirium that has nothing to do with reality. A man is the result of a specific light, a landscape and an atmosphere.*

> *I have always had a passion for what is "concrete". Abstractions and forms have never appealed to me:*
> *I see it - I touch it*
> *I understand it - I love it.*

Gaudí's secret lay in allusions, symbols and signs. All the forms of creation, with the three elements, animal, vegetable and mineral, are the result of the joy of a song sung in stone.

Do you mean that he got his ideas from nature?

Exactly. He was able to select from the infinite number of forms that nature offers us and create a superb synthesis.

> *Nature is a great book of architecture to be studied and learned from.*
> *It is impossible to make anything beautiful unless it is true. The work of art must be beautiful, alive and supported by truth while glorifying God.*

 This is why Gaudí was always an architect, whether he was planning a façade or drawing a window, a seat, a grille, a door-knocker, a table or a chair.

Was he very well known during his life?

I think that, rather than being well-known he was a very controversial man and not well understood. Even today, his buildings are a mystery for many and people make erroneous and sometimes arbitrary assumptions about them.
In fact, it's only now that his fame has spread beyond our borders and he is being studied everywhere. His architecture was never easy and neither was his character or his style. He had to face many obstacles and detractors.

> *I detest the know-alls and mediocrities, the smart alecks who make a point of being ignorant. The cheap critics that only destroy what others create. I detest negative and little people.*

Where did Gaudí come from?

Well, this is also a bit of a mystery because though the books say he was born on 25 June 1852 in Carrer Sant Joan in Reus, others say that he was born on a farm called "Mas de la Calderera" in Riudoms. Either story could be true.

> *When the land is peopled by the warrior band, the farmer is lightning's armour.*

What is sure is that he came from the Tarragona area. He could have been born in Reus or in Riudoms because his parents had houses in both places.
His mother was Antonia Cornet, of Reus. His father was Francesc Gaudí, a boiler-maker from Riudoms.
There is a baptismal certificate, though, dated 26 June 1852 and signed by the parish priest of Saint Peter the Apostle church in Reus, where the child was baptised as Antoni Plàcid Guillem Gaudí i Cornet.

And where did he study?

When he was seventeen, he enrolled at the University of Barcelona to start studying architecture which he did at the city's School of Architecture.
But when he was small he went to a school in the attic of a house in Carrer Monterols in Reus and later to another, of a man named Palau, also in Reus. When he started his secondary studies, his parents sent him to the Reus High School which was then run by the Piarist fathers.

Was he a good student then?

Not totally. It would be truer to say that he was a boy who was indifferent to the marks he obtained. He was an erratic student who, while failing some subjects, did very well in mathematics and the more arts-oriented subjects. The idea of building things was something he saw as a challenge from his early childhood.

There is an anecdote about this. They say that a lady from Reus (mother of the architect Barenys i Gambús), who knew Gaudí as a child, went to Barcelona one day, years later. When she saw the Sagrada Familia, and on being told who had designed it, the woman exclaimed, without any sign of surprise, "But he's doing just the same now as he did when he was little …!"

> *I am a man of space, not of time. That's why I am an architect.*

This sense of construction-space came to him from seeing his father and grandfather working as boilermakers. This led him to seek his solutions in forms and with the spirit of a born observer.

There's another anecdote that illustrates what I've just said. One day the schoolteacher said. "Birds have wings to fly", and the child Antoni answered "The chickens on our farm have got very big wings but they've got no idea how to fly. They use them for running faster." The teacher had no answer for that.

I'd like to be able to visualise him. What was he like?

He had a pleasing, attractive face with penetrating and compelling blue eyes. His forehead and cheekbones were broad. He was of average height with light-brown hair. He didn't gesticulate when he spoke but, if he was interested in the subject, the brightness of his deep gaze betrayed that interest.

He had a strong, impetuous and passionate character. At times he was moody and irascible. He grew more serene, calm and balanced with age, though occasionally he lost his temper. He had a very determined character and it was difficult for him to acknowledge his errors.

In his youth he liked to cut a dash, in keeping with the fashion of the time. He drove around in an open car and visited the building sites without getting out, giving orders and looking at the plans from the seat. He rode horses, was a great gourmet and smoked cigars.

In his old age he was the antithesis of that: unkempt, austere and vegetarian. He only ate salads, milk and dried fruit and nuts and he always had almonds and hazelnuts in his pocket.

> *One has to eat to live, not live to eat. One has to eat and sleep only as much as one needs to survive.*

He loved rambling so he walked a lot. Until he died, his daily walks were a kind of tonic for him.

> *The feet support the head. Walking is essential as a counterbalance to intellectual work and to ensure that one's repose is restorative.*

When his work didn't permit him to walk he received his visitors standing up and didn't sit down all day long as a kind of substitute. He had cold showers in winter and slept all year round with the balcony doors open. He liked working in fresh air and, in the workshop of the Sagrada Familia, he invented a kind of roof that could be raised so that he could see the sun.

This workshop is a cage to catch the sun.

He was a great conversationalist but if he saw that, through distraction, tiredness or lack of interest, he was not being heeded he would stop short with a brusque, "Goodbye!" He always fled from absurd, incoherent and illogical talk.

Only one kind of person can say idiotic things and that's the idiot.

He enjoyed a debate with any amount of persuasive power but not coercion, and he couldn't stand aggressive talk.

Arguments don't shed any light on the matter but only self love.

When he went to study in Barcelona, was he alone? What else did he do apart from studying?

He lived in modest lodgings in Carrer Cadena and later went to Montcada Square, at the end of the street of the same name, to be with his brother Francesc, who was studying Medicine. However, the latter never practised because he died very young. Since his parents weren't very well-off, he had to alternate his studies with working so he became a draftsman for the building supervisor Fontserè, and the architects Emili Sala, Francisco P. de Villar, Joan Martorell and Leandre Serrallach.

He used to go to the workshop of Eudald Puntí as well, and here he learned the carpenter's, blacksmith's, potter's and glass worker's trades. Next to Puntí's workshop, in Carrer de la Cendra, the sculptor and modeller, Llorenç Matamala, had his workshop and here Gaudí soon acquired these two skills. This was very important for him because, in the course of his career, he revealed himself as perhaps more a sculptor than an architect and he always preferred to make clay or plaster models than plans and drawings. And don't forget what I said before, that he regarded himself as "a man of space and not a one-dimensional person".

The boilermaker is a man who, from a flat sheet of metal, has to create volume. Before he begins, he has seen space. The artists of the Florentine Renaissance were stonecutters and they too created volumes from one dimension. There are architects who should know something about boiler-making.

Do you think the place where he was born had an influence on his vision of the nuances of space and colour?

It's difficult to tell. In any case, I'd venture

to say that he felt profoundly Mediterranean and that its light and colour were essential to his work.

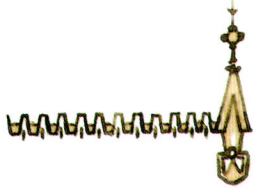

The sun is the great painter of the Mediterranean countries.
The Greeks painted their temples whether they were of simple stone or precious marble. The people in the North don't have this sense of colour in them, but they are very gifted in analysis, science and industry.
Light is the mother of the plastic arts.

Even in his earliest works he played with contrasts – of red tiles, yellow pebbles, the white and green used in ceramics, the black and grey of cast iron.

You can't deceive people. When they see somebody who's very pale, they say, "He looks dead". And when they see somebody who's died with rosy cheeks, they say, "He looks alive".

This intense sense of colour led him to work with stained glass using the three basic colours in order to graduate the intensity of the light. One outstanding example of this is the magnificent stained-glass work in the windows of the Cathedral of Mallorca, representing Saint Ferdinand. This is one of his most successful achievements in this domain.

I challenge anyone, who thinks he can achieve, without the three colours of the glass, the effect of the setting sun's light sliding down over that white horse, to try for himself.

So I think that the wealth of nuances, light and colour that suffuses all his work is thanks to the hundred-per-cent Mediterranean spirit that he so proudly embodied.

What was his first job or project?

Here we need to be a bit specific because Antoni Gaudí was already working on projects when he was a child. Once, when he and his friends Eduard Toda and Josep Ribera were returning from a trip to the monastery of Poblet they conceived the idea of restoring it, and the project was written up in 1870. It is now kept in the library of the monastery of Poblet.
They say that one project he had to do for an exam was the entrance to a cemetery. He immediately produced a coffin to heighten the atmosphere of a funeral and then painted a detailed watercolour of a burial. His teachers didn't understand his mortuary sensibility and failed him. In a new exam he repeated the drawing but this time without adding the burial, highlighting only the entrance in its perfect Romanesque detail. He passed that exam in 1875.
As an architecture student he produced an infinite number of drawings and plans.

In 1876, working with the architect F.P. de Villar, he did a project for the apse of the monastery at Montserrat.
Again, in 1878, before finishing his degree, he participated in different projects, as a draftsman for the Vil·la Arcàdia, a property on Montjuïc in Barcelona, a project for a tram line, the patio of the Diputació (Regional Council) of Barcelona, the General Hospital of Barcelona and a project to make a fountain in the Plaça de Catalunya, also in Barcelona.
The young Gaudí also worked under Fontseré on the waterfall, the Aquarium, and the balustrade of the small square of Vilaseca's monument to Aribau, all in the Ciutadella Park.
On 15 March 1878, Elies Rogent, the head of the School of Architecture, presented him with his degree in Architecture. Rogent is known to have remarked to his colleagues, "I don't know if I have handed the degree to a madman or a genius".

So you can see from all this that he already had experience as an architect before he got his degree.

(On receiving his degree) *"You see, now they say I'm an architect!"*

The first job he did after graduating was sending off to the Paris World's Fair his project for the Mataró Cooperative, after which he worked on the lamp-posts of the Plaça Reial and the Plaça Palau, and his own desk.

The first house he built was the Casa Vicens, in Carrer de les Carolines in Barcelona.

Can you tell us a bit more about his nature-architecture obsession?

Yes and I'll try to do it through talking about his buildings as he conceived them or, in other words, try to approach Gaudí's own way of thinking.
Casa Vicens is a construction with tiles and ceramic decoration where the inspiration is oriental.
The ceramic work has flower patterns and the iron fence around the house is in the form of palmetto leaves.

When I went to measure the site, it was totally covered with little yellow flowers and that's what I used as my ornamental theme.

He also found a big palmetto and he took its leaves and reproduced them in iron to make the fence and entrance gate.
All that is left of the Casa Miralles now is a small wall and the 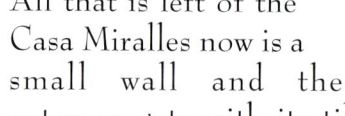 entrance gate with its tiled canopy in the form of a tortoise shell.
"El Capricho" in Comillas has a facade in varnished green and sunflower tiles. The style is oriental, similar to that of Casa Vicens.
The Güell Pavilions: on the column at the entrance, above the "G" for Güell, there are some leaves and wild roses in honour of the Jocs Florals (a literary competition of

which Güell was a leading proponent). Right at the top are four sculpted orange trees crowned by the tree of the golden apple, the mythological one in the garden of the Hesperides. The dragon at the main entrance also gives the feel of a mythological garden to the complex.
With the Plaça Reial lamp-posts he described to perfection the red throat, golden tongue and blue and silver scales of a snake.
The central stained-glass window of Bellesguard represents Venus, the evening star oriented to the west, to the setting sun.
In Güell Park each of the constructions inside this garden-city is a permanent bucolic symbol of nature. The square is perfectly evocative of the undulating sinuosity of a snake; the retaining wall a vivid elemental symbol of palm trees in stone; the Doric Hall or Hall of Columns is a clear homage to the Parthenon, symbol and apogee of Mediterranean architecture, while the fantastic dragon on the stairway seems to be protecting the waters of the pond and, we might say, the whole construction.
Casa Milà ("La Pedrera") is the image of waves beating against the shores of the Cap de Creus. Or a faithful representation of the Artà caves.
Casa Batlló is a marvellous poem in stone to the patron saint of Catalonia, Saint George, and his legend. The dragon, this ferocious beast with its undulating crested back and scales shining into the distance as they reflect the sun, devours anyone who dares to try to free the princess. Their bones, tibiae, fibulae and gloomy skulls are all the dragon has left of them, scattered all over the facade and balconies. Saint George spears it in the back with his sword in the form of the four-branched cross, and kills it. This story is why the house is called "the house of bones".
The balconies also look like masks smiling out from their colourful tones of gold, blue and of lilac, just like flowers blooming in a pond.
And perhaps, as a final example, we can think of the Sagrada Família, Gaudí's most representative work, a skilful interweaving of religious and artistic symbols where the imagination can fly and interpretations of the work can be very different: huge organ pipes, human castles like those created by the group *Xiquets de Valls* — for let us not forget that he was from the Tarragona region ... And there is one quote from Gaudí which makes his intentions very clear ...
One day when he was with his friend Joan Rebull he opened a window which looked out on to the garden of his house and, gazing out with his blue eyes, he exclaimed,

"Those are the towers!"

and he showed his friend the stalks of some acanthus leaves.

Now do you understand the term nature-architecture and why ...

Only in nature is it possible to find the regenerative element of art.

You've told us about his personality and his work but ... who were his friends? Who did he mix with both in and out of the sphere of architecture?

Let's start with the people that were closest to him, his family – his father, mother, his brother Francesc, the one who studied medicine, and his sister Rosa who also died young, not long after she was married, leaving behind the little Rosa who lived with her uncle Antoni until his premature death. There was also a also a sentimental side to Gaudí's life but he never wanted to talk about it. His shyness and his few economic resources may have been why he never settled down to form a family.

I don't have time to think about these things. I've got too much work to do.

His teachers, with whom he worked after he finished his studies, were also good interlocutors for Gaudí and, to a greater or lesser degree, they left their mark on their student's artistic ideas.
But, don't laugh, his best friend was the school library. He skipped a lot of classes because he found them boring and he said he got more from reading books. His avidity to learn about what he didn't understand, his enquiries about the stability of buildings and forms of equilibrium, could only be satisfied if he could study alone.

I don't dare to tell my classmates what I think because I'm afraid they wouldn't believe me.

It was there in the library that he studied, for the first time, Viollet le Duc's Dictionary of Architecture, which was to be the professional model that would most influence his career. His attention was also caught by Arab and Mudejar-style works and the whole polychrome domain.
He was a good friend of the poets Verdaguer and Maragall, the priests Torres i Bages and Jaume Collell, the designers Ruyra and Cerner, the architect Joan Martorell, the Llimona brothers and doctor Pere Santaló.
As I've said, his closest friends were Eduard Toda, Josep Ribera, Salvador Pagès, Alfons Trias i Maixens and Joaquim Bassegoda i Amigó.
And we mustn't forget his patron and friend, Eusebi Güell i Bacigalupi, thanks to whom Antoni Gaudí was able to construct a considerable number of major works.
And again, I don't want to overlook his collaborators, who were essential for him.

I have an idea in my head but I can't see it through alone. I need to be able to delegate.

I need other hands, other minds, people to carry out my ideas. I need to give orders, speak aloud, to speak clearly and frankly. I have become too unconventional to expect to be understood at once.

So, the people who were really close to him, almost all of them architects, were among others:
Josep Mª Jujol i Gibert, who devoted part of his work to Gaudí's mosaics, ceramics and ceramic-fragment designs.
Francesc Berenguer i Mestres, who worked with metal, cast iron, bronze …
Aleix Clapés, painter.
Domènec Sugrañes i Gras, architect.
Carles Mani, sculptor.
Iu Pasqual, stained glass artist.
Llorenç Matamala i Piñol, sculptor.
Ricard Opisso, draftsman and artist who produced drawings.

History is just a man doing things.

And, on the basis of this statement, I tell you myself that these men, these great men, have really made history.

Was he very old when he died?

On 7 June 1926, Antoni Gaudí, at the age of 74 years, left his workshop at the Sagrada Familia to go, as he did every day, to make his evening visit to the chapel of Saint Felip Neri. As usual, he went on foot, giving free rein to his thoughts and absorbed in his ideas. Maybe he was thinking of the day's work or what was to be done the next day.

Vicens, come good and early tomorrow. We've got some great things to do …

He was about to cross the Gran Via de les Corts Catalans, but he wasn't paying attention.
Two trams approached, one in each direction. One of the drivers, the one on line 30, tried to brake and began to ring the bell but … the old man didn't hear a thing. Maybe he was listening to other bells weeping …

The older the bell the better their sound, but they wear out and lose resistance. The final sound of a bell is always the most beautiful.

Perhaps it was that last inner sound that prevented him from hearing the external ringing.

The body of the old man in his shabby clothes and without any documentation ended up under the wheels of the tram. Nobody knew who he was. He was "just another old man".
They took him to the Santa Creu Hospital, which he called the "Holy House".

When his friends found out what had happened, they tried to move him from the poor ward where he had been taken.

My place is here, among the poor.

On 10 June, his lips opened for the last time. *"My God!"* he exclaimed, and his eyes, those intensely blue eyes, then imposed eternal silence.
Antoni Gaudí stopped living but he didn't die because great men never die. They are always present in their works.
The three great loves of Gaudí, God, Catalonia and Architecture are blended together in his work with sensitivity and majesty. His great legacy is one for all of humanity, an offering that will always be present.
As someone once said, through love, symbolised in the Nativity facade, and pain, symbolised in the Passion facade, he longed for triumph, symbolised in the Glory façade.

ANTONI GAUDÍ: an architect who not only has not died, but whose fruits are, and will be, a message for all the future generations.

Antoni Gaudí
i Cornet

Bibliography

ALONSO GAVELA, M.ª J.: *Gaudí en Astorga.* Europa Artes Gráficas, S.A. Salamanca, 1983.
ARCHIVOS DE LA CÁTEDRA GAUDÍ DE LA UNIVERSIDAD POLITÈCNICA DE CATALUNYA.
BASSEGODA I NONELL, J.: *Modernisme a Catalunya,* 1981. Ed. Nou Art. Thor. Barcelona.
BASSEGODA I NONELL, J.: *Gaudí, arte y arquitectura.* Rikuyo-sha. Publishing. Inc. Tokio 1978, 1985.
BASSEGODA I NONELL, J.: *Gaudí.* Gent Nostra, 1981. Ed. Nou Art Thor. Barcelona.
BASSEGODA I NONELL, J.: *Guia de Gaudí.* Ed. Nou Art Thor. Barcelona, 1989.
BASSEGODA, J. y GARRUT, J.M.ª: *Guía de Gaudí,* 1970. Ed. Literarias y Científicas. Barcelona.
BERGOS MASSÓ, J.: *Gaudí, el hombre y la obra.* Univ. Politécnica de Barcelona, 1954, 1974.
BRUGUERA, J.; ILLA, I.; MARQUET, L.; TORRAS, J.: *Diccionari de la Llengua Catalana,* 1987. Enciclopèdia Catalana.
COLET I GIRALT, J.: *El món de les Tercines,* 1988. Ed. Cyan. Barcelona.
COLET I GIRALT, J.: Curs del *Seminari d'Investigació Poètica* (Unpublished treatise) 1988-1989.
COLLIN, G.R.: *Gaudí.* Braziller Ed. New York, 1960.
CONSEJO SUPERIOR DE DEPORTES. *La colombofilia.* Real Federación Colombófila Española. Grafex, S.A. 1982. Madrid.
DE SALA-MORALES, I.: *Gaudí.* Edic. Polígrafa, S.A.
D'ALÒS I MONER, R.: *Autors Catalans Antics,* 1932. Ed. Barcino. Barcelona.
FERRER I PASTOR, F.: *Diccionari de la Rima,* 1980. València.
GRAN ENCICLOPÈDIA CATALANA: Enciclopèdia Catalana, S.A., 1970.
LLAMAZARES, F.: *Astorga y la Maragatería.* Ed. Lancia, S.A. León, 1987.
MARCO, J.: *Antologia Catalana del Segle d'Or,* 1970. Ed. Salvat. Barcelona.
MARTÍN GONZÁLEZ, F.: *La paloma mensajera.* Real Federación Colombófila Española, 1987. Creaciones Gráficas y Publicitarias, S.A., 1987. Madrid.
MASINI, L.V.: *Antonio Gaudí,* 1970. Ed. Nauta, S.A. Barcelona.
MASSÓ I RUHI, M.L. I SUBIRATS, C. I VASSEAUX, P.: *Diccionari invers de la Llengua Catalana,* 1985. Universitat Autònoma de Bellaterra.
MOLAS, J. y MASSOT I MONTANER, J.: *Diccionari de la Literatura Catalana,* 1979. Edicions 62. Barcelona.
MOWER, D.: *Gaudí.* 1977. Oresko Books, Ltel. London.
NAVARRO TOMÁS, T.: *Métrica Española,* 1983. Ed. Labor. Barcelona.
OLIVA, S.: *Mètrica Catalana,* 1980. Quaderns Crema. Barcelona.
PANE, R.: *Antonio Gaudí.* 1983, Edizione di Comunitá Milano.
PERUCHO, J.: *Gaudí, una arquitectura de anticipación.* 1967. Edic. Polígrafo, S.A. Barcelona.
POBLET, J. M.ª: *Gaudí, l'home i el geni,* 1973. Ed. Bruguera, S.A. Barcelona.
POMPEU FABRA: *Gramàtica de la Llengua Catalana,* 1912. l'Avenç. Barcelona.
PUBLICACIÓ DE L'AJUNTAMENT DE BARCELONA, *Guía de Arquitectura de Barcelona,* 1985 Edic. Plaza y Janés, S.A., Barcelona.
RAFOLS, J.F.: *Gaudí,* 1960. Editorial Aedos. Barcelona.
SÁNCHEZ, L.A.: *Breve tratado de Literatura General,* 1939. Ercilla S.A. y Cy Santiago de Chile.
TARRAGÓ, S.: *Gaudí,* 1988. Editorial Escudo de Oro. Barcelona.
TRIADÚ, J.:, *Antologia de la Poesia Catalana,* 1981. Ed. Selecta. Barcelona.
TODO LEÓN Y SU PROVINCIA, Ed. Escudo de Oro, S.A. 1987. Barcelona.

Acknowledgements

First of all, and in particular, we would like to thank the Director of the Gaudí Chair, Professor Joan Bassegoda i Nonell.

Ms. Amèlia Guilera of Bellesguard.

The Reverend Mothers of the Teresian College in Carrer Ganduxer.

All the staff in the technical office of the Sagrada Familia.

Mr. Josep Bobbe of la Pobla de Lillet.

Mr. Francesc Boloix of the Güell Estate.

Ms. Natalia Pujol, Ms. Teresa Sagarra, Ms. Amàlia Gaudí, Ms. Eugenia Martí and Mr. Esteve Núñez de Prado who made it possible for us to gain access to people and entities from the world of Gaudí.

Mr. Ramón Martínez, a pigeon fan and Mr. Lluís Fernández from the Pigeon Lovers' Association of Catalonia.

Ms. Margarida Ruiz and Mr. Antoni Corona, Mr. Lluís Messeguer and Mr. Josep Colet.

Mr. Conrado Quiroga and Mr. Manuel Lorenzana from León.

Mr. José Fernández Pérez from Astorga.

Ms. Rosa Gaudí and her family for their great interest and friendship.

Ms. Àngels Prats and her magic wand.

To

Guida Alzina i Camps

POET AND WRITER
1946 – 2000

THE SONG FEELS THE INFINITE IN THE AIR,
THE PICTURE IN THE EARTH.
THE POEM IN THE AIR AND THE EARTH.
FOR ITS WORDS
HAVE MEANING
AND MUSIC THAT SOARS

                RABINDRANATH TAGORE